THE ASCENT OF F.6

and

ON THE FRONTIER

THE ASCENT OF F.6

and

ON THE FRONTIER

by W. H. Auden *and*
Christopher Isherwood

Faber & Faber Limited
3 Queen Square
London

First published in this edition 1958
by Faber and Faber Limited
3 Queen Square London W.C.1
Reprinted 1966 and 1972
Printed in Great Britain by
Latimer Trend & Co Ltd Whitstable
All rights reserved

ISBN   0 571 06943 6

THE ASCENT OF F.6
a tragedy in two acts

CHARACTERS

This play was first produced on February 26, 1937, *at the Mercury Theatre, by* Ashley Dukes *in association with the Group Theatre. Producer:* Rupert Doone. *Stage Designer:* Robert Medley. *Music by* Benjamin Britten.

Michael Ransom: William Devlin

Sir James Ransom: Raf de la Torre

Lady Isabel Welwyn: Ruth Taylor

General Dellaby-Couch: Erik Chitty

Lord Stagmantle: Edward Lexy

David Gunn: Barry Barnes

Ian Shawcross: Norman Claridge

Edward Lamp: Peter Ashmore

Dr Williams: Philip Thornley

Mrs Ransom: Dorothy Holmes-Gore

The Abbot: Evan John

Mr A.: Will Leighton

Mrs A.: Isobel Scaife

An Announcer: Stuart Latham

Wireless Singers:

Hedli Anderson

Alan Aldridge

Michael Lane

ACT I

ACT I

SCENE I

[*The Summit of the Pillar Rock, above Wastdale. Late afternoon.*]

> [MICHAEL RANSOM *is seated, reading a pocket volume of Dante.*]

RANSOM [*reads*]. 'O brothers!' I said, 'who through a hundred thousand dangers have reached the West, deny not, to this brief vigil of your senses that remains, experience of the unpeopled world behind the Sun. Consider your origin: ye were not formed to live like brutes, but to follow virtue and knowledge.' [*Putting down the book.*] Virtue and knowledge! One can picture Ulysses' audience: a crook speaking to crooks. Seedy adventurers, of whose expensive education nothing remained but a few grammatical tags and certain gestures of the head; refugees from the consequences of vice or eccentric and conceited opinions; natural murderers whom a peaceful winter had reduced to palsied wrecks; the ugly and cowardly who foresaw in a virgin land an era of unlimited and effortless indulgence; teachers without pupils, tormentors without victims, parasites without hosts, lunatic missionaries, orphans.

And glad they must have been to believe it, during the long uneventful voyage westward: yes, even up to the very end, when the last deceptions were choked from each in turn by the strangling Atlantic. Who was Dante—to whom the Universe was peopled only by his aristocratic Italian acquaintances and a few classical literary characters, the fruit of an exile's reading—who was Dante, to speak of Virtue and Knowledge? It was not Virtue those lips, which involuntary privation had made so bitter,

13

could pray for; it was not Knowledge; it was Power. Power to exact for every snub, every headache, every unfallen beauty, an absolute revenge; with a stroke of the pen to make a neighbour's vineyard a lake of fire and to create in his private desert the austere music of the angels or the happy extravagance of a fair. Friends whom the world honours shall lament their eternal losses in the profoundest of crevasses, while he on the green mountains converses gently with his unapproachable love.

Virtue. Knowledge. We have heard these words before; and we shall hear them again—during the nursery luncheon, on the prize-giving afternoon, in the quack advertisement, at the conference of generals or industrial captains: justifying every baseness and excusing every failure, comforting the stilted schoolboy lives, charming the wax-like and baroque, inflaming the obstinate and the odd and all those hungry and cheerful persons whom the holiday now discharges into these lake-filled valleys radiating from the rocky hub on which I sit.

Beyond the Isle of Man, behind the towers of Peel Castle, the sun slides now towards the creasing sea; and it is into a Wastwater utterly in shadow that the screes now make their unhalting plunge. Along the lake shores lovers pace, each wrapped in a disturbing and estranging vision. In the white house among the pines coffee will be drunk, there will be talk of art at the week-end. Under I cannot tell how many of these green slate roofs, the stupid peasants are making their stupid children.

Nevertheless, let me receive such vigour as the impassive embraces of this sullen rock afford, from which no mastery can elicit a gratifying response, nor defeat sighs capable of despairing misinterpretation. Here is no knowledge, no communication, no possession; nothing that a bishop could justify, a stockbroker purchase or an elderly scientist devote years to explaining—only the voluntary homage paid by the living to the unqualified and dangerous dead. Let me pay it, then; pay it now, before I descend to the valley and all its varieties of des-

14

peration: the calculations of shopkeepers under the gas-flares and the destructive idleness of the soldier; the governess in the dead of night giving the Universe nought for behaviour and the abandonment of the prophet to the merciless curiosity of a demon; the plotting of diseases to establish an epoch of international justice and the struggle of beauty to master and transform the most recalcitrant features; the web of guilt that prisons every upright person and all those thousands of thoughtless jailers from whom Life pants to be delivered—myself not least; all swept and driven by the possessive incompetent fury and the disbelief. O, happy the foetus that miscarries and the frozen idiot that cannot cry 'Mama'! Happy those run over in the street today or drowned at sea, or sure of death tomorrow from incurable diseases! They cannot be made a party to the general fiasco. For of that growth which in maturity had seemed eternal it is now no tint of thought or feeling that has tarnished, but the great ordered flower itself is withering; its life-blood dwindled to an unimportant trickle, stands under heaven now a fright and ruin, only to crows and larvae a gracious refuge. . . .

VOICE OF SHAWCROSS [*from below*]. Where are you, M. F.?

VOICE OF GUNN. When you've finished saying your prayers, we should like to go down!

VOICE OF SHAWCROSS. It'll be dark soon, if we don't make a start.

RANSOM [*shouting back*]. All right! I'm coming!

[*He begins to descend as the* CURTAIN *falls.*]

15

[*The* STAGE-BOX, *right, is illuminated.* MRS A. *is discovered cooking.*]

MRS A.   Evening. A slick and unctuous Time
Has sold us yet another shop-soiled day,
Patently rusty, not even in a gaudy box.
I have dusted the six small rooms:
The parlour, once the magnificent image of my freedom,
And the bedroom, which once held for me
The mysterious languors of Egypt and the terrifying Indias.
The delivery-vans have paid their brief impersonal visits.
I have eaten a scrappy lunch from a plate on my knee.
I have spoken with acquaintances in the Stores;
Under our treble gossip heard the menacing throb of our hearts
As I hear them now, as all of us hear them,
Standing at our stoves in these villas, expecting our husbands:
The drums of an enormous and routed army,
Throbbing raggedly, fitfully, scatteredly, madly.
We are lost. We are lost.

[*Enter* MR A. *from work.*]

MR A.   Has anything happened?
MRS A.   What should happen?
The cat has died at Ivy Dene,
The Crowthers' pimply son has passed Matric,
St Neots has put up light blue curtains,
Frankie is walking out with Winnie
And Georgie loves himself. What should happen?
Nothing that matters will ever happen.

16

MR A.   No, nothing that matters will ever happen;
        Nothing you'd want to put in a book;
        Nothing to tell to impress your friends—
        The old old story that never ends:
        The eight o'clock train, the customary place,
        Holding the paper in front of your face,
        The public stairs, the glass swing-door,
        The peg for your hat, the linoleum floor,
        The office stool and the office jokes
        And the fear in your ribs that slyly pokes:
        Are they satisfied with you?
        Nothing interesting to do,
        Nothing interesting to say,
        Nothing remarkable in any way;
        Then the journey home again
        In the hot suburban train
        To the tawdry new estate,
        Crumpled, grubby, dazed and late:
        Home to supper and to bed.
        Shall we be like this when we are dead?

MRS A. It's time for the news, John. Turn on the wireless.

MR A.   I'm sick of the news. All you can hear
        Is politics, politics everywhere:
        Talk in Westminster, talk at Geneva, talk in the
            lobbies and talk on the throne;
        Talk about treaties, talk about honour, mad dogs
            quarrelling over a bone.
        What have they ever done, I ask you? What are they
            ever likely to do
        To make life easier, make life happier? What have
            they done for me or for you?

MRS A. Smiling at all the photographers, smoking, walking
            in top hats down by the lake,
        Treating the people as if they were pigeons, giving
            the crumbs and keeping the cake.
        When will they notice us? When will they flatter
            us? When will they help us? When there's a
            war!

17

	Then they will ask for our children and kill them; sympathize deeply and ask for some more.
Mr A.	Night after night we have listened to the ignoble news.
Mrs A.	We have heard The glib justification of the sorry act.
Mr A.	The frantic washing of the grimy fact.
Mrs A.	But nothing to bring a smile to the face.
Mr A.	Nothing to make us proud of our race.
Mrs A.	Nothing we should have been glad to have done In a dream, or would wish for an only son.
Mr A.	Nothing to take us out of ourselves, Out of the oppression of this city, This abstract civic space imposed upon the fields, Destroying that tie with the nearest which in Nature rules.
Mrs A.	Where we are unable to lose sight of the fruits of our extraordinary industry.
Mr A.	And everything is emphatically provided: The Dial Exchange and the voice of the lift. We must accept them all and there is no one to thank.
Mrs A.	Give us something to be thankful for.
Mr A.	Give it quickly. I have read 'Too Late' in the hands of the office clock.
Mrs A.	I have received singular warnings: In the eyes of the beggar I have experienced the earthquake and the simoom.
Mr A.	Sitting in the crowded restaurant, I have overheard the confabulations of weasels.
Mrs A.	Give us something to live for. We have waited too long.

[*The* STAGE-BOX *is darkened.*]

18

ACT I

SCENE II

[SIR JAMES RANSOM'S *room at the Colonial Office. On the wall at the back of the stage, hangs a large boldly-printed map showing British Sudoland and Ostnian Sudoland, coloured respectively pink and blue. The frontier between the two colonies is formed by a chain of mountains: one peak, prominently marked F6, is ringed with a red circle to emphasize its importance.*]

[*At a table covered with papers, maps and books of reference are seated, from L. to R.* LORD STAGMANTLE, SIR JAMES RANSOM, GENERAL DELLABY-COUCH and LADY ISABEL WELWYN.]
[*As the curtain rises,* JAMES *lays down a document from which he has been reading aloud to the others.*]

JAMES. That, briefly, is the position. I think you'll all agree with me that it is deplorable.

ISABEL. But surely, surely the report exaggerates? My poor darling Sudoland—it's still like home to me, you know! No, I simply can't believe it!

JAMES. We all appreciate your feelings, Lady Isabel. They are most natural. Unfortunately I have reason to believe that this report, so far from exaggerating, may even underestimate the gravity of the situation. . . . From other sources—not official, it is true, but as a rule absolutely reliable—we hear that the whole southern province is in a state of uproar. Government stores have been burnt, British officers have been attacked. In a few hill stations, the women of the European settlements have been grossly insulted——

ISABEL. The cowardly fiends! How they can *dare*! In my father's time——

19

GENERAL. In your father's time, Lady Isabel, a British Governor was required to rule, not to coddle a native population according to the sentimental notions of a gang of home-bred politicians. The Sudoese hillman has not changed since your father's day: take him for what he is, he's a fine fellow. He's a man and he expects to be ruled by men. He understands strength and he respects it. He despises weakness and he takes advantage of it. Show him the business end of a machine-gun and he'll——

JAMES [*acidly*]. I think, General, you can hardly complain that the Government of which I am a member shows any lack of respect for your great practical experience in administration. Otherwise you would not have been invited to attend this conference today. But I should like to suggest that, in your wholesale condemnation of politicians, you are apt to forget that we are only the servants of the public. Public opinion has changed greatly, during the last twenty years, with regard to the native populations of the Empire. There have been unfortunate incidents which unscrupulous party agitators have not hesitated to misrepresent. . . . To take your own case, that most regrettable *contretemps* at Bolo-Bolo. . . .

ISABEL. Really, Sir James, is it necessary, at a time like this, to stoop to personalities?

JAMES [*smoothly*]. My dear Lady Isabel, I'm sure I had no intention of hurting the General's feelings. General, please accept my apologies, I only wished to remind you—not, alas, that any of us need reminding—how grossly a valued public servant can be maligned in the performance of a painful duty by the venom of the popular press——

STAGMANTLE [*beginning to laugh wheezily*]. *British General Butchers Unarmed Mob! Children Massacred In Mothers' Arms! Murder Stains The Jack!*

JAMES [*hastily*]. Yes, yes. . . . The nauseating clichés of gutter socialism——

STAGMANTLE. Socialism my foot! Why, that's out of the *Evening Moon*! Splashed it all over the front page—nearly doubled

20

our sales, that week! No offence, General. We were out to smash the Labour Government, you know: and, by God, we did! Your little stunt came in handy: any stick's good enough to beat a dog with, you know! Ha, ha, ha!

ISABEL. Of all the utterly low and contemptible things I ever heard . . .

JAMES [*hastily intervening*]. As Lord Stagmantle quite rightly observes, the tactical problems raised by a great democratic electorate are exceedingly complex. One must try to see things in perspective. . . . I'm sure nobody doubts Lord Stagmantle's loyalty in this present crisis. Had it not been for his assistance in presenting the events of the last month to the public in their true proportions——

STAGMANTLE. Look here, Ransom; that's just what I came to tell you today. We can't keep this up for ever, you know. *The Thunderbolt* has been featuring the Sudoland revolts now for a week or more. How much longer do you expect us to play hush-hush? It's beginning to affect our circulation already. You've got to do something, quick.

ISABEL. But surely, Lord Stagmantle, all this suppression and misrepresentation of facts is a very mistaken policy? Why can't you have more courage? Why not let the public judge for itself? I should have thought that the truth——

STAGMANTLE. The truth, Lady Isabel, is that the natives of British Sudoland would like us to go to hell—pardon my language—and stay there. The truth is that we've got fifty millions invested in the country and we don't intend to budge—not if we have to shoot every nigger from one end of the land to the other. The truth is that we're under-garrisoned and under-policed and that we're in a blue funk that the Ostnians will come over the frontier and drive us into the sea. Already, they've spent thousands on propaganda among our natives, promising reforms which neither they nor we nor any other colonial power could ever carry out. This revolt is the result. . . . There's the truth for you: and you want me to tell that to the public! What do you take me for—a bolshevik?

JAMES. Lord Stagmantle is perfectly right: though, with his characteristic flair for essentials, he over-simplifies the situation, perhaps, a little. . . . He asks me to do something. I shall not disappoint him. I did not call this meeting merely in order to alarm you. His Majesty's Government has a plan. [*He rises and points dramatically to the map on the wall, indicating F 6.*] The key to the problem lies there!

ISABEL. Why, but that's the Haunted Mountain! I used to be able to see it from my bedroom window at the Residency, when the weather was clear. . . . Let me think, now, what did the natives call it?

JAMES. The mountain has, I understand, many local names; most of them unpronounceable. The survey refers to it simply as F 6.

STAGMANTLE. A haunted mountain, eh? What's the story in it?

JAMES. Merely that the mountain is said to be haunted by a guardian demon. For this reason, no native will set foot upon it. As you will notice, it stands exactly on the frontier line. Both Ostnia and ourselves claim it; but, up to the present, no European has ever visited the district at all.

ISABEL. I remember, when I was a little girl, being afraid that the demon would come and carry me away with him to the top! Aren't children absurd?

GENERAL. May I ask if we came here this morning to discuss fairy-tales?

JAMES. A fairy-tale, General, is significant according to the number of people who believe in it. This one is credited by several millions of natives on both sides of the frontier. . . . Also, the legend has lately developed a sequel which may appeal more strongly to your imagination: The natives have begun telling each other that the white man who first reaches the summit of F 6, will be lord over *both* the Sudolands, with his descendants, for a thousand years.

STAGMANTLE. Aha, so that's their little game! The Ostnians started this yarn, of course?

JAMES. You are very quick to follow me, Lord Stagmantle. And perfectly correct. Yes, the Ostnian agents have been propagating this story for the past six months. We've traced it right down into the plains.

GENERAL. But, Ransom, you don't seriously suggest that the Ostnians expect to gain anything by spreading this absurd nonsense? The hillmen may believe them, I admit—the Sudoese are credulous beggars—but, hang it all, what good can it do Ostnia? None whatever. If you ask me, this is just another Ostnian bluff. Bluffing's their strong suit.

JAMES. I wish I could agree with you, General. But this morning this telegram reached us, through the Intelligence. [*Reads.*] Expedition under Blavek left Ostnia for Ostnian Sudoland yesterday great secrecy intending attempt ascent of F 6.

ISABEL. Monstrous!

GENERAL. The beggars are mad as coots!

STAGMANTLE. Not so mad as you may think, General. I ought to know something about propaganda stunts: this is one of the best I ever struck. If the Ostnians get to the top of F 6, your natives are going to make big trouble. Whether you like it or not, you'll have to start shooting. And Ostnia will intervene, in the name of the poor oppressed subject races. They'll have world opinion on their side, into the bargain. . . . You're in a cleft stick.

ISABEL. Can't we send a cruiser to stop this expedition?

STAGMANTLE. Certainly. If you care to start a European war.

GENERAL. At any rate, these chaps will never reach the summit.

JAMES. We can't be too sure of that, I'm afraid. There's a great deal at stake.

ISABEL. You sit here calmly and say so! Oh, if only I were a man! What are you going to *do*?

JAMES. His Majesty's Government proposes to send an expedition to Sudoland without delay.

ISABEL. Oh, good! Good!

STAGMANTLE. Now you're talking!

GENERAL. Never heard such damned tomfoolery in all my life!

STAGMANTLE. I must congratulate you, Ransom. You're on to a big thing—a big thing for all of us! The *Evening Moon* will subscribe two thousand to the funds of the expedition. . . .

JAMES [*shaking hands with him*]. I knew we could rely on your public spirit, Lord Stagmantle!

STAGMANTLE. . . . provided, of course, that we get the exclusive rights—pictures, film, lecture-tours, story. We can discuss details later. . . .

JAMES [*rather taken aback*]. Er, yes, quite so, of course——

ISABEL. And now, there's not a moment to be lost! We must think quickly: who are you going to send? How will you find the right man to lead them?

JAMES. I am happy to say that I have found him already.

ISABEL. You've found him! Oh, Sir James, I think you're wonderful! Who is he?

JAMES. My brother.

ISABEL. You have a brother! And we never even knew!

JAMES. My brother Michael is considered, by competent experts, to be one of the best climbers in this country.

ISABEL. How I should adore to meet him—the man who can save Sudoland!

JAMES. We'll go to him at once. My car is waiting. [*To* GENERAL *and* STAGMANTLE.] You'll come with us, I hope?

GENERAL. I refuse to be a party to this wild goose chase. When you have ceased to occupy yourselves with demons and need some serious advice, you will find me at my club. Good morning.

ISABEL. Oh, General!

[*The* GENERAL, *taking no notice, goes out.*]

STAGMANTLE. Never mind him, Lady Isabel. . . . A remarkable old gentleman, but conservative: no vision. He'll come round to the idea in time. . . . [*Rubbing his hands gleefully.*] Well, Ransom, let's see this brother of yours! I'll write the interview myself! By George, what a day for the *Evening Moon*!

ISABEL [*reprovingly*]. What a day for *England*, Lord Stagmantle!

STAGMANTLE. Oh, England—yes, quite so, of course. . . .
[*Looking up at map.*] The Ascent of F 6!

> [ALL *three of them stand regarding the map in reverent
> silence as the*——]

CURTAIN FALLS

[The STAGE-BOXES, *left and right, are illuminated. In the right* BOX, MR A. *sits listening to the radio* ANNOUNCER, *who speaks from the* BOX *on the left.]*

ANNOUNCER. If you drink coffee for breakfast, you will be familiar with Sudoland as the name of one of the most delicious brands in the world, said by connoisseurs to be equal even to Blue Mountain and only half the price. But, unless you have a brother or a nephew there, I don't expect you know much more about this beautiful and exciting country. It is about as big as Ireland and embraces a wide variety of scenery and climate, from the moist hot river-plains in the north to the magnificent escarpment of mountains on the southern border. The natives are delightful people, of wonderful physique and very humorous and artistic. Their villages consist of mud huts and they live very simply, chiefly on boiled bamboo shoots, which they call KHA. Most of them are employed on the coffee estates, where they make excellent workmen. You may have read recently, in some of the papers, of riots in Sudoland, but from personal experience I can tell you that these stories have been grossly exaggerated. They were confined to a very small section of irresponsibles egged on by foreign agitators. Hospitals, clinics and schools have done much to raise the standard of personal hygiene and education among the Sudoese and the vast majority are happy and contented.

[At this point, MRS A. *enters the* STAGE-BOX, *right, bringing coffee.]*

If ever I make enough money to retire from journalism, it is to a small hill-station in Sudoland called Fort George that I should like to go, to spend the evening of my days. I have knocked about the world a good deal and seen most of the famous views, but never have I seen anything to compare with the one you get from the English Cemetery

26

there. From this point you see the whole mountain range which culminates in that terrifying fang of rock and ice called so prosaically on our maps 'F 6', but in the native tongue 'Chormopuloda'—that is, the Haunted Mountain. There are many legends about this mountain and the troll who lives on the summit and devours all human beings who dare approach it. No Europeans have, so far, ventured into this region, which is barren to a degree and inhabited only by monks who resent foreigners. These monks practise a mysterious cult which is believed to be descended from the religion of Ancient Egypt; and there are wonderful tales current of their mystical and psychic powers. Be that as it may, I do not think it likely that it will be long before our young climbers will discover a new ground for their sport, offering more magnificent opportunities for their skill and their love of nature, than even those afforded by the Alps or the Himalayas. . . .

[*Exit.*]

MRS A. It's all very well for him, he can travel.

MR A.   Cousin Bertie's boy was there;
    Poor lad, he had to come home last year:
    They've reduced the staff on his coffee estate.
    He said that the people and country were great.

MRS A. Why do you never take me abroad?

MR A.   Darling, you know that we can't afford . . .

MRS A. Afford! It's always the same excuse—
    Money, money!

MR A.   Dear, what's the use
    Of talking like this?

MRS A.   You don't really care;
    If you did, we shouldn't be here.
    Why don't you do something, something that pays;
    Not be a clerk to the end of your days?
    A dreary little clerk on a dreary little screw—
    Can't you find something proper to do?
    But you don't care, it's the same to you
    Whether I live or whether I die.
    I wish I were dead!

MR A.   Mary, don't cry!
           You never know, perhaps one day
           Better luck will come our way:
           It might be tomorrow. You wait and see.
           But, whenever it happens, we'll go on the spree!
           From the first-class gilt saloon of channel-steamer
                we shall peer,
           While the cliffs of Dover vanish and the Calais flats
                appear,
           Land there, take the fastest train, have dinner in the
                dining-car,
           Through the evening rush to Paris, where the ladies'
                dresses are.
           Nothing your most daring whisper prayed for in the
                night alone—
           Evening frocks and shoes and jewels; you shall have
                them for your own.
           Rome and Munich for the opera; Mürren for the
                winter sports;
           See the relics of crusaders in the grey Dalmatian ports;
           Climb the pyramids in Egypt; walk in Versailles'
                ordered parks;
           Sail in gondolas at Venice; feed the pigeons at St
                Mark's. . . .
MRS A. O, what's the use of your pretending?
           As if life had a chance of mending!
           There will be nothing to remember
           But the fortnight in August or early September,
           The boarding-house food, the boarding-house faces,
           The rain-spoilt picnics in the windswept places,
           The camera lost and the suspicion,
           The failure in the putting-competition,
           The silly performance on the pier—
           And it's going to happen again next year!
MR A. Mary!
MRS A.   Don't touch me! Go away! Do you hear?
           [*She bursts into tears; he shrugs his shoulders and
           goes out, slamming the door. The* BOX *is darkened.*]

28

ACT I

SCENE III

[*Parlour of a public house in the Lake District. Shabby late Victorian furniture. A window at the back gives a view towards the fells. By the door, L. is a telephone. On the right, a cottage piano. After supper.*]

> [*At a large table, in the centre of the stage, MICHAEL RANSOM and the DOCTOR are playing chess. At a smaller table, L. LAMP is bending over a microscope. In an armchair, R. SHAWCROSS is writing in a note-book. GUNN is at the piano, strumming and singing. As he writes, SHAWCROSS frowns with suppressed annoyance.*]

GUNN [*singing*]. The chimney sweepers
    Wash their faces and forget to wash the neck;
The lighthouse keepers
    Let the lamps go out and leave the ships to wreck;
The prosperous baker
    Leaves the rolls in hundreds in the oven to burn;
The undertaker
    Pins a small note on the coffin saying 'Wait till I return,
I've got a date with Love!'

And deep-sea divers
    Cut their boots off and come bubbling to the top,
And engine-drivers
    Bring expresses in the tunnel to a stop;
The village rector
    Dashes down the side-aisle half-way through a psalm;
The sanitary inspector
    Runs off with the cover of the cesspool on his arm—
To keep his date with Love!

[*Jumps up from the piano and goes over to* SHAW-
CROSS.]

Still sweating at that old diary?

SHAWCROSS. I was doing my best to, in spite of your filthy row.

GUNN. So glad you enjoyed it, dearie. I'll play you something
else. [*Goes back to piano.*]

RANSOM. Shut up, David. [*To* DOCTOR.] Check.

GUNN [*leaving piano and looking over* SHAWCROSS' *shoulder*].
Hullo, what's all this? [*Reads.*] '. . . followed up a splendid
short pitch to the north summit. Gunn, as usual . . .'

SHAWCROSS [*snatching book*]. Leave that alone, damn you!

GUNN [*grabs book back and reading*]. '. . . Gunn, as usual,
fooling about, completely irresponsible. I can never
understand M. F.'s patience with him. . . .'

[SHAWCROSS *tries to snatch book.* GUNN *dodges round
the chair.*]

SHAWCROSS. Give it here, blast your eyes!

GUNN. Ha, ha! Wouldn't you like it! Why can't you be patient
with me, like M. F.?

SHAWCROSS. You little fool! Do you want me to hurt you?

RANSOM. Give it back, David. [*To* DOCTOR.] Check.

GUNN. Sorry, Ian. You're not cross with me, are you? Come
and have a drink?

SHAWCROSS. Surely you ought to know by this time that I
never drink the day before a climb.

GUNN. To hear you talk, one'd think we were a lot of monks.

SHAWCROSS. It just happens that I take climbing seriously.
You don't.

GUNN. All right. Keep your hair on. No offence. [*Strolls over
to* LAMP.] Let's have a squint, Teddy. [*Looks into micros-
cope.*] What's this stuff that looks like mouldy cheese?

LAMP. If I were to tell you, you wouldn't be any the wiser.

GUNN. No, I expect I shouldn't. [*He wanders over to watch the
chess players.*]

SHAWCROSS. M. F., may I take your climbing boots? I'd like
to oil them for you.

30

RANSOM. It's very kind of you, Ian; but I gave them to the maid.

SHAWCROSS. I wish you wouldn't, M. F. How can you expect a girl to oil boots? I'll just do them over again, myself.

RANSOM [smiling]. You spoil me, Ian. One day, you'll regret it. I shall become as helpless as a baby without its nurse.

SHAWCROSS [blushing]. It's no trouble at all. I like to keep things decent.

GUNN [yawning and stretching himself]. Gosh, I'm bored! If I had a thousand pounds, I'd buy an aeroplane and try to fly across the Atlantic: if I had five hundred pounds, I'd go to Africa and shoot lions. As it is, I've got seven and elevenpence, so I suppose I'd better get drunk.

[As he moves towards the door, the telephone rings.]

SHAWCROSS. I expect that'll be the man about the new ropes. [Goes to telephone.] Hullo. . . . No, it's a call from London. [To GUNN.] For you.

GUNN. Ask who it is. Wait a minute. . . . Don't, for Heaven's sake, say I'm here!

RANSOM [To DOCTOR]. Look out for that castle, Tom.

SHAWCROSS. Who's speaking? [To GUNN.] It's a lady. A Mrs da Silva.

GUNN. Gosh, that's torn it! Tell her I've gone away! Tell her I'm dead!

SHAWCROSS [listening]. She says she knows you're here and that it's no good saying you aren't. [Holding out receiver to GUNN.] Here, take it! I'm not going to do your dirty work for you.

GUNN [after making frantic signals, advances gingerly to the telephone]. Oh, hullo, darling—how lovely to hear your voice! No, of course not! How could you think so! Well, you know, I'm terribly busy just now. I could get up to town this week-end, if it's really absolutely necessary. . . . No, darling, I swear there isn't! Listen, here comes a kiss! Good-bye! [Hanging up receiver and mopping his forehead.] And now she's on the track again! Says her husband's going to divorce her! Oh, whatever shall I do?

SHAWCROSS. I hardly see what else you can expect, when you've got about as much self-control as a tom-cat. . . . What we do object to is the way you involve us all in your nasty little intrigues.

GUNN. Everybody seems to be finding out my address. This morning, I had five more bills. . . . Oh, if only I could get right out of England for six months, they might forget about me.

RANSOM. Check.

DOCTOR [*making a move*]. Aha, M. F., that's got you! . . . No, it hasn't. . . . Oh, dear!

RANSOM. Mate. Thank you, Tom.

DOCTOR. Why do I always do something silly when I play with you? It's no good. You get me every time. [*Rising.*] Oh, I'm so fat, I'm so fat!

GUNN. Doc., I believe you forgot your exercises this morning!

DOCTOR. As if I ever forgot them! As if I ever could forget them! [*Sighs.*] Perhaps it would be better if I stopped them altogether. But I haven't the nerve.

GUNN. Poor old Doc.! Come and have a drink. Whisky shrivels up your flesh.

DOCTOR. Do you really think so? I've got to a stage where I can believe almost anything.

[*A knock at the door.*]

ISABEL'S VOICE. May we come in?

GUNN. Another woman! Don't open it, for the Lord's sake! Let me hide! [*Dives under the larger table.*]

[SHAWCROSS *opens the door. Enter* LADY ISABEL, *followed by* STAGMANTLE *and* SIR JAMES RANSOM.]

ISABEL [*to* JAMES]. I told you they'd be in here!

RANSOM [*unpleasantly surprised*]. James!

JAMES. Ah, Michael, there you are! Very glad to find you at home. I thought I'd pay you a surprise visit. I've brought some friends who were anxious to meet you. . . . May I introduce my brother—Lady Isabel Welwyn, Lord Stagmantle.

RANSOM [*with a rather stiff bow*]. How do you do? These are

my friends—Doctor Williams, Mr Shawcross, Mr Lamp.
. . . David, come out. . . .

[GUNN *scrambles out from under the table.*]

Mr Gunn.

GUNN [*politely*]. How do you do?

JAMES [*to* RANSOM]. I've been telling Lady Isabel and Lord
Stagmantle about your climbing exploits. They were
greatly interested.

ISABEL. You know, Mr Ransom, you're not a bit like Sir
James! I should never have taken you for brothers, at
all!

STAGMANTLE. It's a great pleasure to meet you, Mr Ransom.
I'm always glad to make contacts with prominent personalities, in any walk of life. Sir James tells me that you
have many sidelines. You're a scholar, I believe? Well,
now, that intrigues me. Scholar and man of action: an
unusual mixture, eh?

JAMES. As I never fail to observe, my brother has all the brains
of our family. In all humility I say it—my brother is a
great man.

RANSOM [*who has listened to the above remarks with growing
uneasiness, now turns on* JAMES *and blurts out*]. Why have
you come here? What do you want?

JAMES [*smiling awkwardly*]. Hardly very friendly, are you,
Michael? How do you know that I want anything—
beyond the pleasure of seeing you again after so long?

RANSOM. How often, when we were boys, you used to come
to me as you come today, with that peculiar smile on your
face, half impudent, half timid! What do you want this
time—my toy engine, my cricket bat, my rare West Indian
stamps? Or shall I do you a favour—run that errand to
the butcher's, correct your Latin verses, clean the motor-
bicycle? Let's hear what it is, James: we're grown men
now.

JAMES [*with a change of manner*]. You are quite right, Michael.
I shall not waste words. There is no time to lose. [*Lowering
his voice.*] Isn't it possible for me to speak to you alone?

33

RANSOM. If you have no secrets from your friends, I have none from mine.

JAMES. Very well, since you wish it. . . . [*Clearing his throat.*] In the name of His Majesty's Government, I have come to make you a most important proposition——

RANSOM. Which I unconditionally refuse.

JAMES [*taken aback*]. But—Michael—I haven't even told you what it is!

RANSOM. You have told me quite enough. I know your propositions, James: they are all alike. They are exceedingly convincing. They contain certain reservations. They are concerned with prestige, tactics, money and the privately pre-arranged meanings of familiar words. I will have nothing to do with any of them. Keep to your world. I will keep to mine.

JAMES. You are not being fair to me, Michael. You have never been fair to me. What I am offering you is an opportunity —the greatest of your whole life—to do something after your own heart. We want you to lead an expedition which will attempt the ascent of F 6.

RANSOM [*startled*]. F 6! What have you and your world to do with F 6?

JAMES. Ah, you see, Michael; I told you you would be interested!

RANSOM. Since boyhood, in dreams, I have seen the huge north face. On nights when I could not sleep I worked up those couloirs, crawled along the eastern arête, planning every movement, foreseeing every hold. Through how many thousand years have those virgin buttresses been awaiting me! F 6 is my fate. . . . But not now. Not like this! No, no, no! I refuse!

JAMES. But, Michael, this is sheer caprice! I must explain: the future of England, of the Empire, may be at stake. Weighty political considerations, the Government——

RANSOM. And your own career? Be honest, James, and add the heaviest weight to the scales. . . . No, I am sorry, but F 6 is more important to me even than that. I will not go.

ISABEL. Mr Ransom, if you lead this expedition—no matter whether you succeed or fail: and of course you *will* succeed—there is not a woman in England who will not feel proud of you—*more* than proud! I appeal to you, as an Englishwoman, in the name of all Englishwomen. You refused your brother. Can you refuse *me*?

RANSOM. I can refuse you, Lady Isabel.

ISABEL. You disappoint me, Mr Ransom. Sir James made me hope great things of you. He was too generous. I had never expected this. I see it in your eyes. You are afraid.

RANSOM. I am afraid of a great many things, Lady Isabel. But of nothing which you in your worst nightmares could ever imagine; and of that word least of all.

STAGMANTLE. Look here, Ransom; let's understand each other. I'm not going to talk a lot of blarney to you about England and Idealism. I'm a practical man. You're a practical man—of course you are! Only failures are idealists. My dear fellow, think what this climb will mean to you! Cash, and lots of it! You need cash to pursue your hobby? Of course you do! Look at it in a sensible light. [*Lowers his voice.*] Between ourselves, this expedition's nothing more or less than a political racket. You know that. So do I. Well, who cares! Leave the dirty work to your brother and me: we're used to it. Forget about us. Go out to F 6 and enjoy yourself. Make climbing history. By God, I envy you! If I were twenty years younger, I swear I'd ask you to take me along!

RANSOM. I like your reasons best, Lord Stagmantle. And I respect you. You talk like a man. I'd rather have you in front of me on a rope than behind me with a loud-speaker. . . . I am sorry. I know you won't understand my refusal. But I do refuse.

STAGMANTLE. Is that your last word?

RANSOM. It is.

[*There is a knock at the door.*]

STAGMANTLE. Too bad. . . . Well, Ransom, it seems we shall have to look elsewhere.

JAMES [*triumphantly*]. Not yet! [*He goes to the door, opens it and speaks to someone outside.*] Ah, splendid! So you got my telegram? Yes, he's here!

[*Enter* MRS RANSOM.]

Here is somebody who may be able to persuade you, Michael!

RANSOM [*with a cry of dismay*]. Mother!

MOTHER [*advancing to* RANSOM]. Michael, I am so proud——

RANSOM [*recoiling*]. You too! No, it is impossible!
You come so late, it is an accident
Your shadow adds to theirs, a trick of the light.
If this was purposed——

[*In the course of the following dialogue, the light becomes entirely concentrated upon* RANSOM *and his* MOTHER. *The rest of the stage is darkened: the other figures being seen only as indistinct shapes in the background.*]

MOTHER. I have no purpose but to see you happy,
And do you find that so remarkable?
What mother could deny it and be honest?
I know my son the greatest climber in the world;
I know F 6 the greatest mountain in the world.
May not a mother come at once to bring
Her only gift, her love? When the news came,
I was in bed, for lately
I've not been very well. But what's a headache
When I can stand beside my son and see him
In the hour of his triumph?

RANSOM. If I have triumphed
It is not as you think. I have refused it.

MOTHER. Refused it? Why? But no—I must not question
My grown-up son. You have your reasons, and I
Shall try to trust them always.
James, I remember——

RANSOM.
James! Was there no other name you could remember,
No niece or cousin? Ever since we were born

36

I have heard the note of preference in your voice:
And must I hear it now? When we could barely walk,
I watched him romping through the children's party;
When we were boys at school,
I saw him charm his way to every heart
And idly win the prizes.
That would not matter; we are older now
And I have found myself. But James who has
The gaping world to ogle with his speeches
Must fill the last gap in his great collection
And pot-hunt for his brother. Years ago
He stole my share of you; and must he now
Estrange me even from myself?

MOTHER.   Michael,
There is a secret I have kept so long
My tongue is rusty. What you have said
I knew and I have always known. Why do you start?
You are my Michael and I know my own:
A mother has no heaven but to look.
That was your secret; there is also mine:
From the good day when both of you were born,
And I first held you both in my two arms,
James, bigger, prettier, the doctor's pride,
Responding promptly to the nurse's cluck,
And you, the tiny, serious and reserved,
I knew your natures. You never knew your father:
But I can never see James toss his head
Or laugh, or take a lady's arm, but I
Must see your father in his popular pulpit.
Everyone thought your father wonderful
And so did I, until I married him
And knew him for a shell: James is like him.
He cannot live an hour without applause.
No one can say that I have stinted it.
But you, you were to be the truly strong
Who must be kept from all that could infect
Or weaken; it was for you I steeled my love
Deliberately and hid it. Do you think that it was easy

37

To shut you out? I who yearned to make
My heart the cosiest nook in all the world
And warm you there for ever, so to leave you
Stark to the indifferent blizzard and the lightning?
How many nights have I not bit my pillow
As the temptation fought to pick you out of bed
And cover you with kisses? But I won.
You were to be unlike your father and your brother
You were to have the power to stand alone;
And to withhold from loving must be all my love.
I won, I said—but was the victory real?
There was a mother crucified herself
To save her favourite son from weakness,
Unlike his twin, his brother who depended
Upon the constant praises of the little.
She saved him nothing: he must have them too
Because his brother had them. She had died
To make him free; but when the moment came
To choose the greatest action of his life
He could not do it, for his brother asked him
And he was padlocked to a brother's hatred——

RANSOM. Mother, stop!

MOTHER.   Michael! You mean——?

RANSOM. Yes. Go to James and tell him that you won. And
    may it give him pleasure.

MOTHER. My boy!

> [*She attempts to embrace him. He turns away.*]

BLACK OUT

> [*Music. The darkness is filled with* VOICES *of* NEWS-
> BOYS, *screaming like cats.*]

Evening Special! Evening Special!
Ransom to lead Expedition!
Famous Climber's Decision!
Evening Moon: Late Night Final!
Young English Climber's Daredevil Attempt!
The Haunted Mountain: Full Story and Pictures!
Monasteries in Sudoland: Amazing Revelations!

[*The* STAGE-BOX *on the right is illuminated.* MRS A. *is reading a morning paper.*]

MRS A. I read the papers; there is nothing there
　　　　But news of failure and despair:
　　　　The savage train-wreck in the dead of night,
　　　　The fire in the school, the children caught alight,
　　　　The starving actor in the oven lying,
　　　　The cashier shot in the grab-raid and left dying,
　　　　The young girl slain upon the surgeon's table,
　　　　The poison-bottle with the harmless label,
　　　　The workman fallen in the scalding vat,
　　　　The father's strained heart stopping as he sat,
　　　　The student driven crazy by his reading,
　　　　The roadside accident hopelessly bleeding,
　　　　The bankrupt quaking at the postman's knock,
　　　　The moaning murderer baited in the dock——
　　　　　　　　　　　　[*Enter* MR A. *with evening paper.*]

MR A. Look, Mary! Read this!

　　　　[*As they read,* VOICES *are heard from the darkness of the stage.*]

VOICES. Michael Forsyth Ransom.
　　　　Eight stone six. Aged twenty-eight years.
　　　　Short and blue-eyed.
　　　　His first experiences the rectory elms and the garden quarry.
　　　　Kept a tame rook. Was privately educated,
　　　　By a Hungarian tutor.
　　　　Climbed the west buttress of Clogwyn Du'r Arddu
　　　　While still in his teens. The late Colonel Bow said:
　　　　'That boy will go far.'
　　　　Visited Switzerland; in a single season
　　　　Made a new traverse on the Grandes Jorasses,
　　　　Did the Furggen Shoulder and the Green Needle of Chamonix.
　　　　Studied physiology in Vienna under Niedermeyer.
　　　　Went to the Julian Alps,

Conquered Triglav, mastered the Scarlet Crag.
Disappeared into Asia Minor, appeared in the Caucasus
On two-headed Ushba, returned to England,
In an old windmill near the mouth of the Nen
Translated Confucius during a summer.
Is unmarried. Hates dogs. Plays the viola da gamba.
Is said to be an authority on Goya.
Drinks and eats little but is fond of crystallized
apricots. . . .

[*The* STAGE-BOX *on the left is illuminated.* LORD
STAGMANTLE *is seen at the microphone.*]

STAGMANTLE. It goes without saying that the other members
of the Expedition are the finest flower of English Mountaineering; and, in hands as capable and brilliant as these,
the honour and prestige of Britain, may, I am sure, be
safely left. In this machine-ridden age, some people are
tempted to suppose that Adventure is dead; but the spirit
of Man has never refused to respond to the challenge of
the unknown and men will always be found ready to take
up the gauntlet, mindless of worldly profit, undaunted by
hardship and risk, unheeding the dull spirit which can
only sneer: Cui bono? From such pioneers, the man in
the street may learn to play his part in the great game of
life, small though it may be, with a keener zest and
daring—— [*Exit.*]

[*Meanwhile, the* A.'s *have been cutting photographs
and articles out of the paper and pinning them to the
walls of the box.*]

MR A. Cut out the photos and pin them to the wall,
Cut out the map and follow the details of it all,
Follow the progress of this mountain mission,
Day by day let it inspire our lowly condition.
MRS A.
Many have come to us often with their conscious charms,
They stood upon platforms and madly waved their arms,

40

At the top of their voices they promised all we lack,
They offered us glory but they wanted it back.

Mr A.
But these are prepared to risk their lives in action
In which the peril is their only satisfaction.
They have not asked us to alter our lives
Or to eat less meat or to be more kind to our wives.

[LADY ISABEL *appears at the microphone in the*
STAGE-BOX, *L.*]

ISABEL. The Englishman is reserved. He does not wear his
heart on his sleeve nor put his best goods in his shop-
window. He smokes his pipe and answers in words of one
syllable. So that those who do not know him think that he
is stupid and cold. But every now and then, now in this part
of the world, now in that, something generous, something
brave or beautiful, just happens. And when we start to
investigate it we shall generally find that, at the bottom
of it all, is an Englishman. I have had the privilege of
meeting Mr Ransom and his companions on this expedition personally; and I can say with absolute sincerity
that never in my life have I come away feeling so exalted,
so proud that I belonged to the same country and the same
race as these gallant men. . . . [*Exit.*]

Mrs A. They make no promise to improve our station,
At our weakness they make no show of indignation,
They do not offer contemptuously to lend a hand
But their courage is something the least can under-
stand.

Mr A. The corner tobacconist and the booking-clerk,
The naked miner hewing in the dark,
The forge-hand sweating at the huge steam-hammer,
The girl imprisoned in the tower of a stammer——

Mrs A. The invalid, sheep-counting all the night,
The small, the tall, the black-haired and the white
See something each can estimate,
They can read of these actions and know them great.

41

[GUNN *appears at the microphone in the* STAGE-BOX, *left.*]

GUNN. I don't really know exactly what to say. We none of us know what F 6 is going to be like. If you ask me, I think she's probably an ugly old maid. I'm scared stiff, but Ransom will hold our hands, I expect. . . . We shall be a jolly party; at least, I hope so. I've been on one or two of these expeditions and no one's murdered me yet. They say that there's a ghost at the top; but I've made Doctor Williams promise that if we see anything he'll let me hide behind him. Well, I don't think I've got anything else to say, so I'll tell you a limerick I've just made up:

> There was an old man of F 6
> Who had some extraordinary tricks:
> He took off——

[*An* ANNOUNCER *comes hastily into the* BOX, *pushes* GUNN *aside and speaks into the microphone.*]

ANNOUNCER. We are all most grateful to Mr Gunn for his very interesting talk. Listeners will no doubt join us in wishing the party every success. There will now be a short interval in the programme.

[*Exit* BOTH. STAGE-BOX, *left, is darkened.*]

MRS A. John, I'm so happy! Can't we do something to celebrate?

MR A. Let's go away for the week-end. Let's go now!

MRS A. But it's seven o'clock and supper's nearly ready!

MR A. O, bother the supper! Let it burn!

MRS A. Let's go away and never return;
Catch the last train to——

MR A. Where to?

MRS A. What does it matter?
Anywhere out of this rush and this clatter!
Get your toothbrush, get your pyjamas,
Fetch your razor and let us be gone,
Hurry and pack, may we never come back;
For Youth goes quickly and Age comes on!

42

[THEY *begin to put on their outdoor clothes, pack, etc.*]

MR A.   Dover would like us, Margate would welcome us,
         Hastings and Folkestone would give us a part,
         Hove be excited and Brighton delighted,
         Southend would take us warm to her heart.

BOTH.   Moments of happiness do not come often,
         Opportunity's easy to miss.
         O, let us seize them, of all their joy squeeze them,
         For Monday returns when none may kiss!

[*Exeunt.*]

[*After the A's have departed for Hove, the stage boxes are darkened. A sudden penumbra of light on the stage shows* MRS RANSOM *seated in a high-backed chair facing the audience.*]

MRS RANSOM [*talking to herself in a hoarse and penetrating whisper*]. Michael . . . Michael darling . . . can you hear me? There, there. . . . It's all right. . . . There's nothing to be frightened about. Mother's with you. Of course she won't leave you alone, Michael, never. Wherever you are, whatever you're doing, whether you know it or not, she's near you with her love; for you belong to her always. She's with you now, at sea, on board the ship with your foolish companions, and she'll be with you on the mountain, too. . . . Of course you'll get to the top, darling. Mother will help you. She'll always help you. Wasn't she with you from the very beginning, when you were a tiny baby? Of course she was! And she'll be with you at the very end. . . .

RANSOM [*voice heard, very far off, frightened*]. It's the Demon, mother!

MRS RANSOM [*sings*]. Michael, you shall be renowned,
         When the Demon you have drowned,
         A cathedral we will build
         When the Demon you have killed.
         When the Demon is dead,
         You shall have a lovely clean bed.

You shall be mine, all mine,
You shall have kisses like wine,
When the wine gets into your head
Mother will see that you're not misled;
A saint am I and a saint are you
It's perfectly, perfectly, perfectly true.

BLACK OUT

END OF ACT I

ACT II

ACT II

SCENE I

[*F 6. Room in a Monastery on the Great Glacier. A high, gloomy, vaulted chamber, with doors L. into the courtyard and R. into the interior of the building. In the back wall, arches open into a cloister, beyond which the greenish, faintly glowing ice of the glacier is visible.*]

> [MICHAEL RANSOM *and* SHAWCROSS *are seated at a table in the foreground, on which stand three silver candlesticks with church candles of coloured wax.* RANSOM *and* SHAWCROSS *both have notebooks and pencils; they are checking stores.*]

RANSOM. How many tins of malted milk?

SHAWCROSS. Fifty.

RANSOM. How are we off for pemmican?

SHAWCROSS. Three two-pound tins.

RANSOM. We must remember to ask the monks for yak butter. . . . How about the petrol for the primus?

SHAWCROSS. God, that reminds me! [*He jumps up and goes to the door L. Looks out into the courtyard.*] Two porters haven't finished unloading it *yet*! [*Shouts.*] Hi! Sing ko, pan no ah! Teng fang! Naga! Naga! [*Returns to table.*] Lazy devils! And it'll be dark in a few minutes. . . . That's what comes of leaving things to Gunn. He treats this whole business like a picnic.

> [*He glances quickly at* RANSOM, *who does not, however, respond.*]

RANSOM. Have we got enough soup cubes?

SHAWCROSS. Three large packets. [*Hesitates.*] Look here, M. F., I've been wanting to talk to you about Gunn for a long time now. . . . You know, I hate to bother you with this sort of thing. . . . I've tried to keep you from noticing . . .

RANSOM [*smiles*]. Have you?

SHAWCROSS. You mean, you *did* see something? Well, in a way, I'm glad. Because, if you hadn't, you mightn't have believed me——

RANSOM. I saw that Gunn teased the yaks and scared the porters and played tricks on Tom and Teddy—and on you, too, Ian. I agree that he's often an intolerable nuisance; and I think that without him this expedition would be much more businesslike and very gloomy indeed.

SHAWCROSS [*exasperated*]. The thing I admire most about you, M. F., is your wonderful broadmindedness. It's an example to me. I'm not very tolerant, I'm afraid. If Gunn amused you and the others, I'm glad. I hope I can see a joke as well as anyone. . . . But that wasn't quite what I meant, just now. This is something quite different. I hardly like to tell you——

RANSOM. If you hadn't meant to tell me, Ian, you wouldn't have started this conversation at all.

SHAWCROSS [*blurting it out*]. Well then—Gunn steals!

RANSOM [*laughs*]. Oh, that!

SHAWCROSS. So you *did* know!

RANSOM. I'm surprised that you've only just noticed it. He steals like a magpie; bits of indiarubber, chiefly, but also watches, pencils, and, occasionally, money. . . . That reminds me, I expect he's taken my camera. I was imagining I'd lost it down in the gorge, while we were fording the river.

SHAWCROSS. But, M. F., you can't tolerate this kind of thing! What are you going to do?

RANSOM. Ask him if he's got it.

SHAWCROSS. But surely there's more to it than that? How can you take a man with you who's just a common thief? One has to have some standards of decency, I suppose?

RANSOM [*smiles*]. You haven't changed much, have you, Ian, since you were captain of your school?

SHAWCROSS [*bitterly*]. You're always laughing at me. I suppose you think I'm just a priggish fool?

RANSOM. I certainly don't think you're a fool. You know that I rely on your help more than anybody's to make this expedition a success.

SHAWCROSS. Thank you, M. F. You make me feel ashamed. As long as you trust me, then I don't give a damn what anybody else says or thinks. You know I'd follow you anywhere. We all would. . . . The wonderful thing about a man like you is that you can use all kinds of people and get the best out of each. I think I understand better, now, what it is you get out of Gunn. I don't want to run him down—just because his brand of humour's a bit too subtle for me. [*With increasing bitterness.*] He's not a bad sort in his way; he's all right to have about the place, I suppose, as long as there's no special difficulty or danger. He's a damn good climber, too, I admit—only he simply hasn't got the temperament. I'm wondering what he'll be like up there, on the north face. You remember how he screamed, that day in the Coolins, and wouldn't budge for an hour? It was pitiful.

RANSOM. David's always frightened when he climbs. Otherwise, he wouldn't climb. Being frightened is his chief pleasure in life. He's frightened when he drives a racing-car or seduces somebody's wife. At present he prefers mountaineering because it frightens him most of all.

SHAWCROSS. How well you understand him, M. F.! Now, that's just the point I wanted to make: wouldn't it be better, when we get to Camp A, to leave Gunn behind?

RANSOM [*smiles*]. To damage all the instruments and eat up all the stores?

SHAWCROSS. Well, but, I mean, he'll have to be dropped somewhere, won't he? [*Pause.*] Do you really think it's wise to take him as far as Camp B?

RANSOM. I shall decide when the time comes.

SHAWCROSS. I mean, it's quite settled, isn't it, that only two of us shall try to reach the summit?

RANSOM. Yes. There'll be only two of us.

49

SHAWCROSS. And you can't, for a moment, be thinking of taking Gunn? [*Pause.*] My God, it'd be madness! M. F.— you couldn't!

RANSOM. Have I said I shall?

SHAWCROSS [*with growing excitement*]. If I thought such a thing was possible, I'd—I don't know what I'd do! Gunn, that miserable little rotter! Why, he's not a climber at all! He's just a neurotic! He poses. He does everything for effect! Just a beastly little posing coward! [*Pause.*] Oh, I know you think I'm simply jealous!

[*Enter* LAMP *and the* DOCTOR, *L.*]

LAMP [*excited*]. The flora here is amazing, simply amazing! I've had one of the most wonderful afternoons of my life! I tell you what, Doctor—— [*Sees the others.*] Oh, here you are, M. F.! Didn't see you in the dark.

[SHAWCROSS *silently lights the candles.*]

I was just telling the Doctor, I've had a field-day! Extraordinarily interesting! M. F., I'm convinced that Hawkins is wrong when he denies the possibility of a five-leaved Polus Naufrangia! And what's more, I don't mind betting you I shall find one here, on F 6.

RANSOM. Let's see what you got this afternoon.

LAMP [*opens his vasculum*]. Here's Stagnium Menengitis and Frustrax Abominum. . . . Isn't it a beauty! And look here, here's something to surprise you: you told me there wasn't a Rossus Monstrens with blue petals! Well, what do you say to this?

RANSOM [*examines flower*]. This is interesting.

[*Enter* GUNN. *L.*]

GUNN. Ah, here you all are! Thank goodness! I've been hunting for you everywhere! I began to think something had happened to you. . . . [*Sits down and mops his forehead.*]

DOCTOR. What's the matter with you, David? You look rattled.

GUNN. You'd be rattled if you'd been hanging round this place all the afternoon. Ugh! It gives me the creeps!

DOCTOR. Why, what's wrong with it?

GUNN. Those beastly monks. . . . Don't they make you feel damned queer, with those cowls over their faces? I've been watching them for hours, out there: they never seem to speak or make any signs; they just stand facing each other, like this—and yet you have a nasty sort of feeling that they're talking, somehow. . . . I shouldn't wonder if they do it by telepathy or something.

DOCTOR. They seemed quite friendly and harmless when we arrived.

GUNN. Don't you believe it. . . . They're plotting to do us in while we're asleep, I bet you they are. . . . This afternoon, when I was sitting watching the porters unload, I kept imagining there was somebody standing just behind me. Several times I turned round quickly to try and catch him, but there was nothing there. . . . And then I saw a monk and I thought I'd ask him which room we could use for the stores. So I went over to him and made signs and he seemed to understand all right. He turned round and went to one of the doors and opened it and went inside. Naturally, I followed him. But when I got into the room, there was nobody there. And there wasn't even a window he could have got out of. . . . No, I don't like this place!

DOCTOR. I tell you what, David, you've had a touch of the sun. I'll give you something to make you sleep well tonight.

RANSOM. Oh, by the way, David, where's my camera? You've got it, haven't you?

GUNN [*with a charming smile*]. Yes. It's in my room. I thought I'd look after it for you for a bit.

SHAWCROSS. Well, of all the blasted——!

RANSOM. That was very kind of you. Would you bring it here now, please?

GUNN. Very well—if you'd rather——

[*As he moves towards the door, L., a low chanting begins from the courtyard outside. This chant continues throughout the following scene. Its words are:*]

51

Go Ga, morum tonga tara
Mi no tang hum valka vara
So so so kum mooni lara

Korkra ha Chormopuloda
Antifora lampisoda
Kang ku gar, bari baroda

Ming ting ishta sokloskaya
No rum ga ga, no rum gaya
Nong Chormopuloda sya.

GUNN. My God! What's that? [*Retreats hastily behind* RANSOM's *chair.*]

SHAWCROSS [*goes to door L. and looks out*]. They're all gathered out there in the courtyard. They're starting a procession. Now they're beginning to go round in circles. They've got torches and banners. . . .

GUNN. Lock that door, for Heaven's sake! Suppose they come in here!

SHAWCROSS. Do you ever think of anything except your own beastly little skin?

[*Meanwhile the others have joined him at the door.* GUNN *comes last, unwillingly, curious in spite of himself.*]

DOCTOR. From the way they walk it might be a funeral.

LAMP. I believe it *is* a funeral. Look what they're carrying.

GUNN. A coffin! Gosh, did you see?

DOCTOR. Cheer up, David; there's only one! Perhaps they won't choose you.

GUNN. It's most likely some wretched traveller they've murdered.

DOCTOR. Very curious, those masks. A pity it's too dark for a photograph.

SHAWCROSS. Now they're going. I wonder where that door leads to? Probably into the temple precincts.

[*The chanting dies away.*]

LAMP [*as they close the door and return downstage to the table*]. What did you make of it, M. F.?

52

RANSOM. I've read about these rites, somewhere. They're supposed to propitiate the spirits which guard the house of the dead.

GUNN. Anyhow, I hope there won't be any more! Phew! This place is about as cheerful as Woking Cemetery!

[*As he speaks, the door on the R. opens noiselessly and a cowled* MONK *enters, carrying in his hands a crystal which glows faintly with a bluish light.*]

You chaps didn't really think I was scared, did you? I was only ragging. It takes more than a few old monks to frighten *me*! [*Turns and suddenly sees the* MONK. *Screams.*] Oh, God!

[*As the* MONK *advances towards the front of the stage,* GUNN *retreats backwards before him.*]

What does he want? Help! Do something, somebody! M. F., you speak to him!

RANSOM. Om no hum, no na num se? [*Pause.*] No num seng ka, gang se gang? [*Pause.*] King t'sang po, ka no ah? [*Pause.*] Either he doesn't understand any of the three hill-dialects, or he isn't allowed to answer.

DOCTOR. Funny kind of a lamp he's got there. [*Approaches.*]

GUNN. I say! Do be careful! He may have a knife up his sleeve!

DOCTOR. Extraordinary thing—it doesn't seem to be a lamp at all. It just shines. [*Bends over the crystal.*] Why, it's a kind of mirror—I can see myself in it! Am I really as fat as that? Gracious, I'm quite bald! Hullo, what's this? I'm sitting in an armchair. I seem to know that room. . . . Yes, it's the Reform Club! I say, I think I must have got a touch of the sun like David. Am I just seeing things? Here, Teddy, you come and look!

LAMP [*looks*]. Polus Naufrangia! As plain as anything: all five leaves. By Jove, what a beauty! [*Rubs his eyes.*] I must be going mad!

GUNN. He's hypnotizing you, that's what it is! When we're all in a trance, we shall probably be murdered. . . . I say, I must have a look!

53

LAMP [*excited*]. I saw it as plain as that candle! Five distinct leaves!

GUNN [*looks*]. Why, there's my old Alfa Romeo! And some-one's sitting in it—it's a woman, dressed all in black! She seems to be at a cross-roads. I see the sign-post, but I can't read what's written on it. . . . Now she's turning her head. My God, it's Toni—Mrs da Silva! [*Comes away.*] Do you think that means her husband's died and now she'll follow me out here? Come on, Ian. Your turn!

SHAWCROSS [*takes a pace towards the crystal, stops, bursts out violently*]. I'm not going to have anything to do with this damned business! You others please yourselves. It isn't right. We aren't meant to know these things. [*Calmer.*] It's probably some kind of trick, anyhow. . . . M. F., I'm going to get the wireless ready. It's nearly time to pick up the weather report from Fort George. [*Takes up one of the candles and exits, L.*]

GUNN. You'll have a look, won't you, M. F.?

RANSOM [*hesitates a moment*]. Very well. [*Looks into crystal.*]

> [*As he does so, voices are heard from the darkened stage-boxes.*]

VOICES.

Give me bread	Restore my dead
I am sick	Help me quick
Give me a car	Make me a star
Make me neat	Guide my feet
Make me strong	Teach me where I belong
Strengthen my will	Make me still
Make me admired	Make me desired
Make me just	Cool my lust.

54

[*Together*].

Make us kind
Make us of one mind
Make us brave
Save
Save
Save
Save.

DOCTOR. Well, what is it this time? Motors or flowers or London clubs?

GUNN. Try and see something useful. Ask it to tell you the best route up F 6.

RANSOM [*after a long pause*]. I can see nothing.

GUNN. Nothing at all? Oh, M. F.!

DOCTOR. That all goes to support your hypnotism theory. M. F. was a bit too strong for him.

[*The* MONK *turns silently and goes out by the door, R.*]

GUNN. Ought we to have tipped him, or anything? Gosh, you know, that crystal has given me quite a headache! I can't understand your not seeing anything, M. F. Or was it so awful that you won't tell us?

DOCTOR. I feel I could do with a change of air. Let's go and see if Ian's got Fort George.

GUNN. Right you are. Coming, M. F.?

RANSOM. No. I'll stay here. The Abbot may wish to speak to me.

[GUNN *and* DOCTOR *go out, L.*]

RANSOM. Bring back the crystal. Let me look again and prove my vision a poor fake. Was it to me they turned their rodent faces, those ragged denizens of the waterfronts, and squealed so piteously: 'Restore us! Restore us to our uniqueness and our human condition.' Was it for me the prayer of the sad artist on the crowded beaches was indeed intended? 'Assassinate my horrible detachment. My love for these bathers is hopeless and excessive. Make me

55

also a servant.' I thought I saw the raddled sick cheeks of the world light up at my approach as at the home-coming of an only son. . . . How could I tell them that?

[*Enter the* ABBOT *and* TWO ACOLYTES, *R.*]

ABBOT [*makes sign of benediction*]. Only God is great.

RANSOM [*kneels and kisses his hand*]. But His power is for mercy.

ABBOT. I hope everything has been arranged to your satisfaction?

RANSOM. It is perfect.

ABBOT. I am glad. Please be seated, Mr Ransom. Will you do me the honour of taking a glass of wine with me? In these mountains, I fear we can offer but poor hospitality, but I think you will not find this wine totally unworthy of your palate. Your health, Mr Ransom.

[*Toast.*]

[*The* ACOLYTES *exeunt R.*]

Now tell me. You wish to start soon on your ascension of our mountain?

RANSOM. Tomorrow. If He permit it, Whose will must be done.

ABBOT. You know the legend?

RANSOM. I have read the Book of the Dead.

ABBOT. Such interest, Mr Ransom, is uncommon in one of your race. In that case, you will have comprehended the meaning of the ceremony that was performed this evening out in the courtyard: the office for the souls of the dead and the placation of the Demon. I am afraid that you, with your western civilization, must consider us here excessively superstitious. . . . No, you need not contradict me out of politeness. I understand. You see the painted mask and the horns and the eyes of fire and you think: 'This Demon is only a bogey that nurses use to frighten their children: I have outgrown such nonsense. It is fit only for ignorant monks and peasants. With our factory chimneys and our furnaces and our locomotives we have banished these fairy-tales. I shall climb the mountain and

56

I shall see nothing.' But you would be wrong. The peasants, as you surmise rightly, are simple and uneducated; so their vision is simple and uneducated. They see the truth as a crude and coloured picture. Perhaps, for that reason, they see it more clearly than you or I. For it is a picture of truth. The Demon is real. Only his ministry and his visitation are unique for every nature. To the complicated and sensitive like yourself, Mr Ransom, his disguises are more subtle. He is—what shall I say?—the formless terror in the dream, the stooping shadow that withdraws itself as you wake in the half-dawn. You have heard his gnashing accusations in the high fever at a very great distance. You have felt his presence in the sinister contours of a valley or the sudden hostility of a copse or the choking apprehension that fills you unaccountably in the middle of the most intimate dinner-party. I did you an injustice just now when I said that you expected to see nothing on the mountain. You do expect to see something. That is why you are intending to climb it. You do not make that foolish, that terrible mistake so common among your fellow-countrymen of imagining that it is fortunate to be alive. No. You know, as I do, that Life is evil. You have conquered the first temptation of the Demon, which is to blind Man to his existence. But that victory exposes you to a second and infinitely more dangerous temptation; the temptation of pity; the temptation to overcome the Demon by will. Mr Ransom, I think I understand your temptation. You wish to conquer the Demon and then to save mankind. Am I right?

RANSOM. So you know of my vision in the crystal?

ABBOT. Ah, you saw it there, too? That is not strange. For all men see reflected there some fragment of their nature and glimpse a knowledge of those forces by whose free operation the future is forecast and limited. That is not supernatural. Nothing is revealed but what we have hidden from ourselves; the treasures we have buried and accursed. Your temptation, Mr Ransom, is written in your face. You know your powers and your intelligence. You could ask the world to follow you and it would serve you with blind obedience; for most men long to be delivered from the terror of thinking and feeling for themselves. And yours is the nature to which those are always attracted in whom the desire for devotion and self-immolation is strongest. And you would do them much good. Because men desire evil, they must be governed by those who understand the corruption of their hearts, and can set bounds to it. As long as the world endures, there must be order, there must be government: but woe to the governors, for, by the very operation of their duty, however excellent, they themselves are destroyed. For you can only rule men by appealing to their fear and their lust; government requires the exercise of the human will: and the human will is from the Demon.

RANSOM. Supposing you are right. Supposing I abandon the mountain. What shall I do? Return to England and become a farm labourer or a factory hand?

ABBOT. You have gone too far for that.

RANSOM. Well then——

ABBOT. There is an alternative, Mr Ransom; and I offer it you.

RANSOM. What?

ABBOT. To remain here and make the complete abnegation of the will.

RANSOM. And that means——?

ABBOT. You saw the corpse in the procession?

RANSOM. Yes.

ABBOT. In the course of your studies you have become acquainted, no doubt, with the mysteries of the rites of Chöd? The celebrant withdraws to a wild and lonely spot and there the corpse is divided and its limbs scattered. The celebrant, sounding on his bone trumpet, summons the gluttonous demons of the air to their appointed feast. At this moment there issues from the crown of his head a terrible goddess. This goddess is his Will, and she is armed with a sword. And as the ghouls of the mountain and of the sky and of the waters under the glacier

58

assemble to partake of the banquet, the goddess with her sword cuts off the limbs of the celebrant's esoteric body, scatters them and apportions his entrails among the demon guests. And the celebrant must wish them good appetite, urging them to devour every morsel. These rites, Mr Ransom, are so terrible that frequently the novices who witness them foam at the mouth, or become unconscious or fall dead where they stand. And yet, so tedious is the path that leads us to perfection that, when all these rites have been accomplished, the process of self surrender can hardly be said to have begun. . . . Well, Mr Ransom, I must leave you now. Do not make up your mind at once. Think my proposal over.

RANSOM. Before you go, may I ask you a question? As Abbot, you rule this monastery?

ABBOT. That is a wise observation. Mr Ransom, I am going to tell you a secret which I have never told a living soul. We have spoken of your temptation. I am now going to tell you of mine. Sometimes, when I am tired or ill, I am subject to very strange attacks. They come without warning, in the middle of the night, in the noon siesta, even during the observance of the most sacred religious rites. Sometimes they come frequently, sometimes they do not occur for months or even years at a time. When they come I am filled with an intoxicating excitement, so that my hand trembles and all the hairs on my body bristle, and there comes suddenly into my mind strange words, snatches of song and even whole poems. These poems sing always of the same world. A strange world. The world of the common people. The world of blood and violent death, of peasant soldiers and murderers, of graves and disappointed lust. And when I come to myself again and see these monastery walls around me, I am filled with horror and despair. For I know that it is a visitation of the Demon. I know that, for me, nothing matters any more: it is too late. I am already among the lost. Good-night, Mr Ransom.

[*Exit R.*]

RANSOM. Is it too late for me? I recognize my purpose. There was a choice once, in the Lakeland Inn. I made it wrong; and if I choose again now, I must choose for myself alone, not for these others. Oh, You who are the history and the creator of all these forms in which we are condemned to suffer, to whom the necessary is also the just, show me, show each of us upon this mortal star the danger that under His hand is softly palpitating. Save us, save us from the destructive element of our will, for all we do is evil.

[*Enter* GUNN, *L.*]

GUNN. You alone? Good. I was afraid I might be butting in; but Ian and the others threw me out. And I didn't much like the idea of sitting by myself in the dark, with all those monks around. [*Pause.*] Are you busy, M. F.? Would you rather I didn't talk?

[RANSOM *is deep in his thoughts. He doesn't answer.* GUNN, *after regarding him for a moment in silence, begins again.*]

The wireless is coming through beautifully. No atmospherics at all. I heard the weather report; first class. We'll be able to start tomorrow for a cert.

RANSOM. You sound pleased.

GUNN. Of course I'm pleased! Who wouldn't be—after all these weeks of messing about? Tomorrow we shall be on the ice!

RANSOM. Tell me, David; what is it that makes you so keen to climb this mountain?

GUNN [*laughs*]. What is it that makes one keen to climb any mountain?

RANSOM. F 6 is not like any mountain you have ever climbed.

GUNN. Why not? It's got a top, hasn't it? And we want to get to it, don't we? I don't see anything very unusual in that.

RANSOM. You've thought enough about the ascent of F 6 no doubt; about the couloirs and the north buttress and the arête. . . . Have you thought about the descent, too: the

60

descent that goes down and down into the place where Stagmantle and my Brother and all their gang are waiting? Have you thought about the crowds in the streets down there, and the loudspeakers and the posing and the photographing and the hack-written articles you'll be paid thousands to sign? Have you smelt the smell of their ceremonial banquets? Have you loathed them, and even as you were loathing them, begun to like it all? [*Becomes hysterically excited.*] Have you? Have you?

GUNN [*scared*]. M. F., what on earth do you mean?

RANSOM. Don't lie to me now, David. Are you corrupt, like the rest of us? I must know. [*Seizes* GUNN *by the wrists and stares into his face.*] Yes. Yes. I see it! You too. How horrible! [*Throws him violently aside.*] Get out of my sight!

> [*Enter* SHAWCROSS, DOCTOR *and* LAMP: *all far too excited to notice that anything unusual has been happening.*]

SHAWCROSS. M. F.! A message has just come through: Blavek and his party are on the mountain already!

GUNN. But it's impossible! When we last heard, he was still on the other side of the Tung Desert!

SHAWCROSS. Well, this is official. He must have been making forced marches. These fellows aren't mountaineers at all —they're soldiers! There's a whole regiment of them! Do you know, M. F., what they're doing? They're hammering the whole south face full of pitons and hauling each other up like sacks! Good God, they'll be using fire-escapes before they've finished! Well, that settles it! We haven't a moment to lose!

RANSOM. And you are all anxious to play their game: the race to the summit? This won't be mountaineering. It'll be a steeplechase. Are you so sure the prize is worth it? Ian, you're the purist: is this your idea of climbing? No time for observations; no time for reconnoitre. Teddy, hadn't you better stay out of this? We can't wait a week, you know, while you look for your flowers.

61

LAMP. I'll take my chance of that later. We've got to beat
    Blavek!

RANSOM. Blavek is only another victim of the mountain. And
    you, Tom?

DOCTOR. You don't expect me to stay here, do you, M. F.?
    Why, this makes me feel twenty years younger already!

RANSOM. You, too. . . . Stagmantle's latest convert. He should
    be honoured.

SHAWCROSS. What's the point of all this talk? The people in
    England expect us to get to the top before the Ostnians.
    They believe in us. Are we going to let them down?

GUNN. I think this makes it all the more exciting. Good old
    Blavek!

RANSOM. Very well then, since you wish it. I obey you. The
    summit will be reached, the Ostnians defeated, the Empire
    saved. And I have failed. We start at dawn. . . .

CURTAIN

[*The* STAGE-BOX *on the right is illuminated. The* A.'s
are having breakfast.]

MRS A. Give me some money before you go
There are a number of bills we owe
And you can go to the bank today
During the lunch-hour.

MR A.   I dare say;
But, as it happens, I'm overdrawn.

MRS A. Overdrawn? What on earth have you done
With all the money? Where's it gone?

MR A. How does money always go?
Papers, lunches, tube-fares, teas,
Tooth-paste, stamps and doctor's fees,
Our trip to Hove cost a bit, you know.

MRS A. Can we never have fun? Can we never have any
And not have to count every single penny?
Why can't you find a way to earn more?
It's so degrading and dull to be poor.
Get another job.

MR A.   My job may be small
But I'm damned lucky to have one at all.
When I think of those I knew in the War,
All the fellows about my age:
How many are earning a decent wage?
There was O'Shea, the middle-weight champion;
    slouches from bar to bar now in a battered hat,
    cadging for drinks;
There was Morgan, famous for his stories; sells
    ladies' underwear from door to door;
There was Polewhele, with his university education;
    now Dan the Lavatory Man at a third-rate
    night-club;
And Holmes in our office, well past fifty, was dis-
    missed last week to bring down expenses;

63

Next week another: who shall it be?
It may be anyone. It may be me.

[*A newspaper is dropped through the door into the back of the Box.* MR A. *goes to fetch it.*]

MRS A. It's all this foreign competition:
Czechoslovakia, Russia, Japan,
Ostnia and Westland do all they can
To ruin our trade with their cheap goods,
Dumping them on our market in floods.
It makes my blood boil! You can find
No British goods of any kind
In any of the big shops now.
The Government ought to stop it somehow——

MR A. Listen to this. [*Reads.*] Our Special Correspondent reports that the Ostnian Expedition to F 6, headed by Blavek, has crossed the Tung Desert and is about to commence its final assault on the mountain. Blavek is confident of success and, in mountaineering circles, it is believed that the British climbers will have to make very strenuous efforts indeed if they are to beat their formidable opponents. . . .

MRS A. You see? The foreigner everywhere,
Competing in trade, competing in sport,
Competing in science and abstract thought:
And we just sit down and let them take
The prizes! There's more than a mountain at stake.

MR A. The travelogue showed us a Babylon buried in sand.

MRS A. And books have spoken of a Spain that was the
brilliant centre of an Empire.

MR A. I have found a spider in the opulent board-room.

MRS A. I have dreamed of a threadbare barnstorming actor,
and he was a national symbol.

MR A. England's honour is covered with rust.

MRS A. Ransom must beat them! He must! He must!

MR A. Or England falls. She has had her hour
And now must decline to a second-class power.

[*Puts on his bowler hat and exit, brandishing his newspaper. The* STAGE-BOX *is darkened.*]

ACT II

SCENE II

[*On F 6. At the foot of the West Buttress. The back of the stage rises slightly, suggesting a precipice beyond. A magnificent panorama of distant mountains. On the right of the stage, the wall of the buttress rises, with an overhang.*]

> [*Midday.* RANSOM, SHAWCROSS *and* LAMP *stand roped on the edge of the precipice, assisting the* DOCTOR *and* GUNN, *who are still out of sight, below. The rope is belayed round a rock.*]

RANSOM [*looking down*]. There's a hold to your left, Tom. No, a little higher up. Good. Now you're all right.

GUNN'S VOICE [*from below*]. Look out, Doc.! Don't tread on my face!

RANSOM. Now then. . . .

> [*After a moment, the* DOCTOR *hoists himself into view, panting.*]

Now you take it easy, Tom. Fifteen minutes' rest, here.

LAMP. We've made good time, this morning.

RANSOM [*looking down*]. You all right, David?

GUNN'S VOICE [*from below*]. I think so. . . . No! Ooh, er! Gosh, this rock is soft! Here we come!

> [*He appears.*]

DOCTOR. Well, thank goodness, that couloir's behind us, anyhow. Though how we shall ever get down it again is another matter.

RANSOM. You were splendid, Tom. Never known you in better form.

DOCTOR. I must have lost at least two stone. That's one comfort.

65

GUNN. While we were in the chimney, I felt his sweat dripping on to me like a shower-bath. . . . I say, isn't there anything more to eat?

RANSOM. I'm afraid we must keep to our rations, David. We're only carrying the minimum, you know.

SHAWCROSS. I should have thought you'd eaten enough to satisfy even *your* appetite—considering you had all my chocolate, as well.

GUNN. Well, you needn't make a grievance out of it. You didn't want it, did you?

DOCTOR. Still feeling sick, Ian?

SHAWCROSS [*crossly*]. I'm all right.

DOCTOR. You don't look any too good.

SHAWCROSS. Anyhow, I don't see that it helps much to keep fussing about trifles and thinking of one's comfort.

[*A pause.*]

LAMP. Well, if we've got another ten minutes to spare, I think I'll be taking a look round. Might spot a clump of Polus Naufrangia. You never know. It's about the right altitude, now.

[*He goes to the back of the stage and looks over, through his binoculars.*]

GUNN [*following him*]. See anything?

[LAMP *shakes his head.*]

Gosh, that's a drop! [*He balances on the edge and pretends to wobble.*] Ooh, er! Help!

RANSOM. Come away from there, David.

[GUNN *obeys and begins wandering about the stage.*]

DOCTOR [*pointing upwards*]. How high do you make that buttress?

RANSOM. About seventeen hundred feet. We shall be on it all this afternoon. We ought to reach the ridge easily by sunset.

66

GUNN [*poking about*]. Hullo, what's this? [*Picks up a skull.*]
Doctor Livingstone, I presume?

[*The others, except* LAMP, *who continues to peer through his binoculars, collect round* GUNN.]

How on earth did he get here?

DOCTOR. Goodness knows. May have fallen from above. See this crack? It's hardly likely to have been murder, up here.

SHAWCROSS. Anyhow, he must have been a pretty useful climber to have got as far as he did. I suppose there's no doubt it's a native skull?

DOCTOR. Impossible to say. It may have been some mad European who thought he'd have a shot at F 6 on his own; but that's scarcely possible. Some herdsman, probably. . . . What do you think, M. F.?

[*Hands him the skull.*]

LAMP [*shouting excitedly*]. Come here! Look!

GUNN. What's the matter, Teddy?

LAMP. Polus Naufrangia! Five-leaved! A beauty! Only just spotted it. And it was right under my nose!

[*He begins lowering himself over the edge.*]

DOCTOR. Wait a moment, Teddy. Better do that on the rope.

GUNN [*looking over*]. He'll be all right. It's a broad ledge. Only about twenty feet down.

DOCTOR [*looking over*]. Careful, Teddy. Careful. Take your time.

LAMP'S VOICE [*from below*]. I'm all right.

[*The others, except* RANSOM, *stand looking over the edge*].

RANSOM [*to skull*]. Well, Master; the novices are here. Have your dry bones no rustle of advice to give them? Or are you done with climbing? But that's improbable. Imagination sees the ranges in the Country of the Dead, where those to whom a mountain is a mother find an eternal playground. There Antoine de Ville scales pinnacles with subtle engines; Gesner drinks water, shares his dreams with Saussure, whose passion for Mont Blanc became a kind of illness. Paccard is reconciled with Balmont, and Bourrit, the cathedral precentor, no longer falsifies their story. Marie-Coutett still keeps his nickname of The Weasel; Donkin and Fox are talking of the Caucasus; Whymper goes climbing with his friends again and Hadow, who made the slip of inexperience, has no faults. While, on the strictest buttresses, the younger shadows look for fresher routes: Toni Schmidt is there and the Bavarian cyclists; and that pair also whom Odell saw on the step of Everest before the cloud hid them for ever, in the gigantic shadow of whose achievement we pitch our miserable tent——

[*The roar of an approaching avalanche is heard.*]

DOCTOR. An avalanche! My God!

[RANSOM *runs to join the others.*]

Look out, Teddy! Look out!
GUNN. Quick, man!
SHAWCROSS. Stay where you are!
GUNN. Jump for it!
DOCTOR. Oh, God! He's done for!

[*The roar of the avalanche drowns their voices; then gradually dies away.*]

SHAWCROSS. He was just stooping to pick the flower, when the first stone got him.
DOCTOR. It was all over in a moment. He was probably knocked right out.
SHAWCROSS. As he went over the edge, you could see the flower in his hand.
GUNN. Gosh, I feel beastly!

[*Sits down on a rock.*]

68

SHAWCROSS. He was a damn good man!

DOCTOR. I'm glad he found the Naufrangia, anyway. We must tell them that in London. Perhaps the five-leaved kind will be named after him. He'd like that, I think.

SHAWCROSS. I just can't believe it. Five minutes ago, he was standing here.

DOCTOR [*looking at* LAMP'S *rucksack, which is lying on a rock.*] What do you think we ought to do with this? His people might like to have it.

SHAWCROSS. We can't very well take it with us now. I think we'd better bury it here. We can pick it up on our way down.

DOCTOR. Right you are. I'll help you. [*Begins collecting stones.*]

[SHAWCROSS *picks up the rucksack.*]

GUNN. Poor old Teddy! [*To* SHAWCROSS.] Half a minute! [*Feels in the pocket of the rucksack.*] Oh, good!

[*Pulls out a piece of chocolate and begins eating it.*]

SHAWCROSS [*horrified*]. My God! Haven't you any decency left in you at all?

GUNN [*with his mouth full*]. Why, what's the matter now?

SHAWCROSS. Of all the filthy callousness!

GUNN. But, honestly, I don't see anything wrong. He doesn't want it now, does he?

SHAWCROSS. If that's the line you take, I suppose there's no more to be said. . . . Get some stones!

[*While the others are burying the rucksack,* RANSOM *stoops and picks up* LAMP'S *snow-glasses, which he has left lying on the rocks at the back of the stage.*]

RANSOM. The first victim of my pride. If I had never asked him, he would not have come. The Abbot was perfectly right. My minor place in history is with the aberrant group of Caesars: the dullard murderers who hale the gentle from their beds of love and, with a quacking drum, escort them to the drowning ditch and the death in the desert. . . . [*To the others.*] You have forgotten these.

[*Gives glasses.*] Hurry up. We must be getting on. Ian, will you change places with David?

[*Music. They rope up in silence.* RANSOM *begins the traverse round the buttress, as the* CURTAIN *slowly falls.*]

[*Both* STAGE-BOXES *are illuminated. In the left-hand box,* STAGMANTLE *is at the microphone. In the right-hand box, the* A.'s *sit, listening. Mr A. is playing Patience.* MRS A. *is darning socks.*]

STAGMANTLE. It is with the deepest regret that we have to announce the death of Mr Edward Lamp, a member of the F 6 Expedition. He was climbing along a ridge on the north face after a rare botanical specimen when he was caught by an avalanche and killed. He was twenty-four years of age.

In Edward Lamp, Science has lost one of her most brilliant recruits. At Cambridge he carried everything before him; and his career, so tragically cut short, promised to be of the highest distinction. He died as he had lived: in the service of his austere mistress. This is as he would have wished; and no man can do more. Nor could one design him a more fitting grave than among the alpine flowers he loved so passionately and with such understanding. . . . [*Exit.*]

MRS A. [*moved*].

Death like his is right and splendid;
That is how life should be ended!
He cannot calculate nor dread
The mortifying in the bed,
Powers wasting day by day
While the courage ebbs away.
Ever-charming, he will miss
The insulting paralysis,
Ruined intellect's confusion,
Ulcer's patient persecution,
Sciatica's intolerance
And the cancer's sly advance;
Never hear, among the dead,
The rival's brilliant paper read,

71

Colleague's deprecating cough
And the praises falling off;
Never know how in the best
Passion loses interest;
Beauty sliding from the bone
Leaves the rigid skeleton.

Mr A. If you had seen a dead man, you would not
Think it so beautiful to lie and rot;
I've watched men writhing on the dug-out floor
Cursing the land for which they went to war;
The joker cut off half-way through his story,
The coward blown involuntary to glory,
The steel butt smashing at the eyes that beg,
The stupid clutching at the shattered leg,
The twitching scarecrows on the rusty wire;
I've smelt Adonis stinking in the mire,
The puddle stolid round his golden curls,
Far from his precious mater and the girls;
I've heard the gas-case gargle, green as grass,
And, in the guns, Death's lasting animus.
Do you think it would comfort Lamp to know
The British Public mourns him so?
I tell you, he'd give his rarest flower
Merely to breathe for one more hour!
What is this expedition? He has died
To satisfy our smug suburban pride. . . .

[*The* STAGE-BOXES *are darkened.*]

72

ACT II

SCENE III

[*On F 6. CAMP A. The left of stage is occupied by a tent, which is open at the end facing the audience. Behind it, to the right, the ground rises to a platform of rock, overhanging a precipice. It is early evening: during the dialogue which follows, the stage slowly darkens. Wind noises.*]

[RANSOM *and the* DOCTOR *are inside the tent, preparing a meal. The* DOCTOR *is cooking on the Primus stove.*]

DOCTOR. The wind's getting up again. It's going to be a bad night. . . . I wish those two would turn up.

RANSOM. We can't expect them just yet. They're loaded, remember; and the going isn't easy.

DOCTOR. What was the psychrometer reading?

RAMSON. 6·5.

DOCTOR. We're in for a lot more snow.

RANSOM. It looks like it.

DOCTOR. And if it's bad down here, what's it going to be like up there on the arête?

RANSOM [*smiling*]. Worse.

DOCTOR. M. F.—you can't start tomorrow!

RANSOM. I must.

DOCTOR. If you try it in this weather, you haven't a chance!

RANSOM. We shall have a better chance tomorrow than the day after. Three days from now, there'd be none at all. We can't hang on here for more than four days: we haven't the stores.

DOCTOR. To try the arête in a blizzard is sheer madness!

RANSOM. Hasn't this whole climb been madness, Tom? We've done things in the last week which ought to have been planned and prepared for months. We've scrambled up here somehow, and now we must make a rush for it. . . . Whatever the weather is, I must leave for the summit tomorrow.

DOCTOR. Very well, M. F. You didn't bring me up here to argue with you. I won't. Just tell me what you want me to do.

RANSOM. Today is Tuesday. You'll wait for us here till Friday, at dawn. If we aren't back by then, you'll descend at once to Camp B, rest there as long as necessary and then carry out the evacuation of the mountain, as we arranged. . . . You understand, Tom? At once. There is to be no delay of any kind.

DOCTOR. You mean: no search party?

RANSOM. Nothing. If you like, I'll put that in writing. I forbid all useless risks. [*Smiling.*] I order you to return to England alive.

DOCTOR [*smiling*]. You'd better repeat that order to David personally.

RANSOM. David?

DOCTOR. He'll be second in command now, I suppose?

[RANSOM *looks at him, smiles slightly and is silent.*]

Michael—you aren't thinking of taking him with you to the summit?

RANSOM. What if I am?

DOCTOR. Then you've chosen already?

RANSOM. Please don't question me now, Tom. Perhaps I have chosen. Perhaps I haven't, yet. We'll speak about it later. I can't tell you any more now.

DOCTOR. Very well, Michael. Just as you wish.

[*A pause.*]

RANSOM. I know what you're thinking. Ian is steady, reliable, a first-class climber: David is only a brilliant amateur, a novice with an extraordinary flair, unsound, uneven, liable to moments of panic, without staying power. Yes, it's all true.

74

DOCTOR. Ian's wanted to do this climb with you more than he's ever wanted to do anything in his whole life.

RANSOM. I know. I've felt that, often. All these weeks, he's been on edge, straining every muscle and every nerve, never relaxing, torturing himself, denying himself, watching me like a dog waiting for a sign. . . . Already he's utterly exhausted; he's a feverish invalid. Take this sickness of his: as long as I've known him, Ian's never been sick on a mountain before. . . . You see, Tom, the ascent of F 6 represents, for Ian, a kind of triumph which he not only desires but of which he's desperately afraid. He can't face it. He wants me to order him to face it. But if I do, it will destroy him.

DOCTOR [after a pause]. Perhaps you're right, M. F. . . . Yes, I think you are. But surely—you've admitted it yourself—David is afraid, too?

RANSOM. David is afraid of precipices, avalanches, cornices, falling stones. He is afraid of being killed; not of dying. He is not afraid of F 6, nor of himself.

DOCTOR. M. F.—The boys have their whole lives before them. Take me.

RANSOM [after a pause]. Yes, I'd thought of that, too. Thank you for asking me, Tom. I am very honoured.

DOCTOR. Oh, I know it's impossible, of course. I'm a fat old man. The crystal was right: I shall die in my bed.

RANSOM. You will die at the end of a long and useful life. You will have helped a great many people and comforted all whom you could not help. . . . But the Demon demands another kind of victim——

[Whistling from GUNN, off. Enter GUNN and SHAW-CROSS, R. Both of them are carrying stores. They cross the stage and enter the tent.]

GUNN. Hullo, M. F.! Hullo, Doc.! Are we late for supper?

DOCTOR. No, it's just ready now.

[GUNN and SHAWCROSS put down their loads. SHAW-CROSS is much exhausted: GUNN fresh and lively. RANSOM lights the tent lantern.]

GUNN. Gosh, I'm hungry! The altitude doesn't seem to affect *my* appetite. What is there to eat?

DOCTOR. Cocoa and oatmeal. [*Hands round rations.*]

GUNN. Oatmeal again!

DOCTOR. Perhaps you'd prefer a mutton chop?

GUNN. Don't, Tom, you swine! You make my mouth water! The first thing I'll do when I get back, I'll stand you dinner at Boulestin's. We'll start with two dozen Royal Whitstable's——

DOCTOR. Oh, but David, Danish are much better!

GUNN. Just as you like. What about soup? Minestrone, I think?

DOCTOR. You have that. I prefer a really good tomato to anything.

GUNN. And now, what would you say to Lobster Newberg?

DOCTOR. I oughtn't to, really; but I can't resist.

GUNN. Good Lord! We've forgotten the wine!

SHAWCROSS [*bitterly*]. Must you always be talking about food?

GUNN. Was I? Sorry.

SHAWCROSS. Well, for God's sake, shut up then!

[*A pause.*]

DOCTOR. You're not eating anything, Ian.

SHAWCROSS. I don't wany any, thanks.

DOCTOR. Take just a little. You must eat something, you know.

SHAWCROSS [*angrily*]. You heard me say No once. Are you going deaf?

RANSOM. Doctor's orders, Ian.

SHAWCROSS. All right, M. F. If you say so——

RANSOM [*handing him his mug of cocoa*]. Try this. It's good.

[SHAWCROSS *sips listlessly, putting the mug down almost at once.*]

GUNN. Thank God for my good dinner! Please may I get down? [*Pretending to strum on mandolin, sings:*]
Some have tennis-elbow
And some have housemaid's knee,
And some I know have got B.O.:
But these are not for me.

76

There's love the whole world over
Wherever you may be;
I had an aunt who loved a plant—
But you're my cup of tea!

DOCTOR [*laughing and applauding*]. Bravo!

[GUNN *bows.*]

You know, M. F., this reminds me of our first climb together, on the Meije. Do you remember that hut?

RANSOM. And our Primus that wouldn't light? Shall I ever forget it?

DOCTOR. And the fleas in the straw? Extraordinary the altitudes fleas can live at! Funny things, fleas. . . . If a flea were as big as a man, it could jump over St Paul's.

GUNN. When I was at school, I tried to keep a flea circus. But I could never train them to do anything at all. They're not really very intelligent.

DOCTOR. Perhaps you didn't go the right way about it. A man told me once that if——

SHAWCROSS [*passionately*]. Oh, for Christ's sake, shut up!

DOCTOR. Why, what's the matter, Ian?

SHAWCROSS. Do you expect me to sit listening to your drivel the whole night? Why do we keep pretending like this? Why don't we talk of what we're all thinking about? M. F., I've had about as much of this as I can stand! You've got to tell us now: which of us are you taking with you tomorrow?

DOCTOR. Steady, Ian! [*Puts a hand on his arm.*]

SHAWCROSS [*shaking him off*]. Let me alone, damn you! I wasn't talking to you! M. F., you've bloody well got to choose!

RANSOM. I have chosen, Ian. I'm taking David.

SHAWCROSS. Oh, my God! [*Pause.*] And I knew it all the time!

GUNN. Rotten luck, Ian. . . . I say, let me stay behind. . . . I don't mind, so very much. . . .

SHAWCROSS [*shouting*]. My God, do you think I'm going to crawl for favours to *you*, you little swine. You were always his favourite! I don't know how I've kept my hands off you so long! [*He tries to throttle* GUNN: *the* DOCTOR *seizes* him.]

DOCTOR. Ian, that's enough!

SHAWCROSS [*struggling free*]. Oh, I know—you're on his side, too! Do you think I haven't heard you whispering behind my back?

RANSOM. Is this what all your talk of loyalty amounts to, Ian? Tom and David have nothing to do with this. I am in charge of this expedition. If you have anything to complain of, be man enough to say so to me.

SHAWCROSS. I'm sorry, M. F. Forgive me. You're quite right. I'm no damn good: I realize that now. You're all better men than I am. I had a pretty fine opinion of myself, once. I imagined I was indispensable. Even my admiration of you was only another kind of conceit. You were just an ideal of myself. But F 6 has broken me; it's shown me what I am—a rotten weakling. . . . I'll never give orders to anybody again.

RANSOM. No, Ian. You're wrong. F 6 hasn't broken you. It has made a man of you. You know yourself now. Go back to England with Tom. One day you will do something better worth while than this fool's errand on which David and I are going. I am giving you a harder job than mine.

SHAWCROSS [*hesitating*]. If I only could——! But you don't really believe it: I see you don't! No one will ever—— [*With rising excitement.*] They'd look at me and think—— No, I couldn't bear it! He failed—I can't—no, no—— I'll never let them! Never!

[*He turns to rush out of the tent.*]

DOCTOR. Ian! [*They struggle at the tent flap;* SHAWCROSS *breaks free and runs across to the rock above the precipice; the others following.*]

RANSOM. Stop him!

GUNN. Ian, you fool, come back!

> [SHAWCROSS, *with a loud cry, springs over the preci-pice. The others reach the rock and stand peering down into the darkness. Gale noises and music.*]

CURTAIN

[*In the right-hand Box, the* A.*'s are listening.* MRS A. *is adjusting the wireless:* MR A. *stands restlessly cleaning his pipe. In the left-hand Box, the* AN-NOUNCER *is at the microphone.*]

ANNOUNCER. There is still no news of the British Expedition to F 6. Fort George reports that a severe blizzard is general over the whole range. The gravest anxiety is felt as to their safety——

MR A. Turn off the wireless; we are tired of descriptions of travel;

    We are bored by the exploits of amazing heroes;

    We do not wish to be heroes, nor are we likely to travel.

    We shall not penetrate the Arctic Circle.

    And see the Northern Lights flashing far beyond Iceland;

    We shall not hear the prayer from the minaret echoing over Arabia.

    Nor the surf on the coral atoll.

MRS A. Nor do we hope to be very distinguished;

    The embossed card of invitation is not for us;

    No photographers lurk at our door;

    The house-party and the grouse-moor we know by hearsay only;

    We know of all these from the lending library and the super cinema.

MR A. They excite us; but not very much. It is not our life.

MRS A. For the skidding car and the neighbours' gossip

    Are more terrifying to us than the snarling leap of the tiger;

80

And the shop-fronts at Christmas a greater marvel
    than Greece.

MR A.   Let our fears and our achievements be sufficient to
    our day.

MRS A. The luck at the bargain counter:

MR A.   The giant marrow
    grown on the allotment.

MRS A. Our moments of exaltation have not been extra-
    ordinary
    But they have been real.

MR A.   In the sea-side hotel, we experienced genuine passion:

MRS A. Straying from the charabanc, under tremendous
    beeches.
    We were amazed at the profusion of bluebells and
    the nameless birds;
    And the Ghost Train and the switchback did not
    always disappoint.

MR A.   Turn off the wireless. Tune in to another station;
    To the tricks of variety or the rhythm of jazz.
    Let us roll back the carpet from the parlour floor
    And dance to the wireless through the open door.

[*They turn on the wireless and a dance band is heard.
The A.'s leave the box.*]

ANNOUNCER [*sings*].
    Forget the Dead, what you've read,
    All the errors and the terrors of the bed;
    Dance, John, dance!
    Ignore the Law, it's a bore,
    Don't enumer all the rumours of a war;
    Dance, John, dance!
    Chin up!
    Kiss me!
    Atta Boy!
    Dance till dawn among the ruins of a burning Troy!

    Forget the Boss when he's cross,
    All the bills and all the ills that make you toss:

Dance, John, dance!
Some get disease, others freeze,
Some have learned the way to turn themselves to trees;
Dance, John, etc.

> [*The* STAGE-BOXES *are darkened.*]

ACT II

SCENE IV

[*On F 6. The Arête. Hurricane. Late afternoon.* RANSOM *supporting* GUNN.]

RANSOM. Steady. Lean on me.

GUNN. No, it's no use. I can't go any further. Help me down there, out of this bloody blizzard. [*They descend to a ledge.*] [*Collapsing.*] Thanks. But hurry. Go on, now, and reach the top. F 6 is a household word already. The nursemaids in the park go into raptures. The barber's chatter's full of nothing else. You mustn't disappoint them. In London now, they are unlocking the entrances to tubes. I should be still asleep but not alone. Toni was nice but very difficult. . . . Now no policeman will summons me again for careless driving. . . . They're flagging from the pits. . . . I cannot stop. . . . The brakes are gone. . . . Ian would be feeling as sick as a cat. . . . Where is that brake? Two hundred. . . . Christ, what banking! [*Dies.*]

RANSOM.

You always had good luck; it has not failed you
Even in this, your brightest escapade,
But extricates you now
From the most cruel cunning trap of all,
Sets you at large and leaves no trace behind,
Except this dummy.
           O senseless hurricanes,
That waste yourselves upon the unvexed rock,
Find some employment proper to your powers,
Press on the neck of Man your murdering thumbs
And earn real gratitude! Astrologers,
Can you not scold the fated loitering star
To run to its collision and our end?

83

The Church and Chapel can agree in this,
The vagrant and the widow mumble for it
And those with millions belch their heavy prayers
To take away this luggage. Let the ape buy it
Or the insipid hen. Is Death so busy
That we must fidget in a draughty world
That's stale and tasteless; must we still kick our heels
And wait for his obsequious secretaries
To page Mankind at last and lead him
To the distinguished Presence?

CURTAIN

[*The* STAGE-BOXES *remain darkened. A voice from each is heard, in duet. They are like people speaking in their sleep.*]

LEFT BOX.	RIGHT BOX.
No news	
	Useless to wait
Too late	
	Their fate
	We do not know
Snow on the pass	
	Alas
Nothing to report	
	Caught in the blizzard
Fought through the storm	
	Warm in our beds we wonder
Thunder and hail	
	Will they fail? Will they miss their success?
Yes. They will die	
	We sigh. We cannot aid
They fade from our mind	
	They find no breath
But Death	

ACT II

SCENE V

[*F 6. The stage rises steeply, in a series of rock terraces, to the small platform at the back which forms the summit of the mountain. Blizzard. Gathering darkness.*]

[*In the front of the stage* RANSOM *is struggling upwards. After a few numbed movements, he falls exhausted. Music throughout. The light now fades into complete darkness. The voices of the* CHORUS, *dressed in the habit of the monks from the glacier monastery, are heard.*]

CHORUS.

Let the eye of the traveller consider this country and weep,
For toads croak in the cisterns; the aqueducts choke with leaves:
The highways are out of repair and infested with thieves:
The ragged population are crazy for lack of sleep:
Our chimneys are smokeless; the implements rust in the field
And our tall constructions are felled.

Over our empty playgrounds the wet winds sough;
The crab and the sandhopper possess our abandoned beaches;
Upon our gardens the dock and the darnel encroaches;
The crumbling lighthouse is circled with moss like a muff;
The weasel inhabits the courts and the sacred places;
Despair is in our faces.

[*The summit of the mountain is illuminated, revealing a veiled, seated figure.*]

For the Dragon has wasted the forest and set fire to the
    farm;
He has mutilated our sons in his terrible rages
And our daughters he has stolen to be victims of his
    dissolute orgies;
He has cracked the skulls of our children in the crook of
    his arm;
With the blast of his nostrils he scatters death through
    the land;
We are babes in his hairy hand.

O, when shall the deliverer come to destroy this dragon?
For it is stated in the prophecies that such a one shall
    appear,
Shall ride on a white horse and pierce his heart with a
    spear;
Our elders shall welcome him home with trumpet and
    organ,
Load him with treasure, yes, and our most beautiful
    maidenhead
He shall have for his bed.

> [*The veiled* FIGURE *on the summit raises its hand.
> There is a fanfare of trumpets. The* DRAGON, *in the
> form of* JAMES RANSOM, *appears. He wears full cere-
> monial dress, with orders. He is illuminated by a spot-
> light. The* CHORUS, *throughout the whole scene,
> remain in semi-darkness.*]

> [*As* JAMES *appears, the* CHORUS *utter a cry of dismay.*
> JAMES *bows to the* FIGURE.]

JAMES. I am sorry to say that our civilizing mission has been
subject to grave misinterpretations. Our critics have been
unhelpful and, I am constrained to add, unfair. The
powers which I represent stand unequivocally for peace.
We have declared our willingness to conclude pacts of
non-aggression with all of you—on condition, of course,
that our demands are reasonably met. During the past

few years we have carried unilateral disarmament to the utmost limits of safety; others, whom I need not specify, have unfortunately failed to follow our example. We now find ourselves in a position of inferiority which is intolerable to the honour and interests of a great power; and in self-defence we are reluctantly obliged to take the necessary measures to rectify the situation. We have constantly reiterated our earnest desire for peace; but in the face of unprovoked aggression I must utter a solemn warning to you all that we are prepared to defend ourselves to the fullest extent of our forces against all comers.

[JAMES *is seated. Duet from the darkened* STAGE-BOXES.]

DUET.   Him who comes to set us free
         Save whoever it may be,
         From the fountain's thirsty snare,
         From the music in the air,
         From the tempting fit of slumber,
         From the odd unlucky number,
         From the riddle's easy trap,
         From the ignorance of the map,
         From the locked forbidden room,
         From the Guardian of the Tomb,
         From the siren's wrecking call,
         Save him now and save us all.

[*Flourish on the wood-wind.* MICHAEL RANSOM *steps into the light which surrounds the Dragon* JAMES. *He still wears his climbing things but is without helmet, goggles or ice-axe.*]

AMES. Michael! Why have you come here? What do you want?

RANSOM. Hardly very friendly, are you?

JAMES. What is it this time? We are grown men now.

RANSOM. There is no time to lose. I have come to make you a most important proposition.

JAMES. Which I accept—on my own conditions.

[*At his signal a complete set of life-size chessmen appear. The chief pieces on* JAMES' *side are* STAGMANTLE, ISABEL *and the* GENERAL; *and on* MICHAEL'S, SHAWCROSS, GUNN *and* LAMP. *All have masks which partially disguise them.*]

Before we continue, if any of you have any questions you would like to put either to my colleagues or myself, we shall be delighted to do our best to answer them.

[*As each character answers his question, he or she removes the mask.*]

MR A. [*from stage-box*]. Why is my work so dull?

GENERAL. That is a most insubordinate remark. Every man has his job in life, and all he has to think about is doing it as well as it can be done. What is needed is loyalty, not criticism. Think of those climbers up on F 6. No decent food. No fires. No nice warm beds. Do you think *they* grumble? You ought to be ashamed of yourself.

MRS A. Why doesn't my husband love me any more?

ISABEL. My dear, I'm terribly sorry for you. I do understand. But aren't you being just a teeny-weeny bit morbid? Now think of those young climbers up there on F 6. They're not worrying about their love affairs. [*Archly.*] And I'm sure they must have several. Of course, I know people like you and me can't do big things like that, but we can find little simple everyday things which help to take us out of ourselves. Try to learn Bridge or get a book from the lending library. Reorganize your life. I know it won't be easy at first, but I'm sure if you stick to it you'll find you won't brood so much. And you'll be ever so much happier.

MR A. Why have I so little money?

STAGMANTLE. Ah, I was expecting that one! I'm a practical man like yourself, and as it happens I'm a rich one, so I ought to know something about money. I know there are far too many people who have too little. It's a damned shame, but there it is. That's the world we live in. But

89

speaking quite seriously as a business man, I can tell you that money doesn't necessarily bring happiness. In fact, the more you worry about it, the unhappier you are. The finest and happiest man I ever met—he's leading the expedition up F 6 at the moment—doesn't care a brass button for money, and never has. So my advice is: Get all the cash you can and stick to it, but don't worry.

MR A. and }
MRS A. } Why were we born?

JAMES. That's a very interesting question, and I'm not sure I can answer it myself. But I know what my brother, the climber, thinks. When we take, he said to me once, the life of the individual, with its tiny circumscribed area in space and time, and measure it against the geological epochs, the gigantic movements of history and the immensity of the universe, we are forced, I think, to the conclusion that, taking the large view, the life of the individual has no real existence or importance apart from the great whole; that he is here indeed but to serve for his brief moment his community, his race, his planet, his universe; and then, passing on the torch of life undiminished to others, his little task accomplished, to die and be forgotten.

RANSOM. You're not being fair to me.

JAMES. Keep to your world. I will keep to mine.

[*The chess game begins. Complete silence, accompanied only by a drum roll. At intervals* JAMES *or* MICHAEL *says: 'Check!'*]

JAMES. Check!

RANSOM [*looking for the first time towards the summit and seeing the figure*]. Look!

JAMES. Mate! I've won!

[*The* FIGURE *shakes its head.*]

RANSOM [*his eyes still fixed upon it*]. But was the victory real?

JAMES [*half rises to his feet, totters: in a choking voice*]. It was

90

not Virtue—it was not Knowledge—it was Power!
[*Collapses.*]

CHORUS. What have you done? What have you done?
You have killed, you have murdered her favourite son!

[*Confusion. During the following speeches,* STAG-
MANTLE, *the* GENERAL *and* ISABEL *jostle each other,
jump on each other's shoulders to get a better hearing
and behave in general like the Marx brothers.*]

STAGMANTLE. The whole of England is plunged into mourning
for one of her greatest sons; but it is a sorrow tempered
with pride, that once again Englishmen have been weighed
in the balance and not found wanting.

ISABEL. At this hour, the thoughts of the whole nation go out
to a very brave and very lonely woman in a little South
country cottage; already a widow and now a bereaved
mother.

GENERAL. I am no climber; but I know courage when I see it.
He was a brave man and courage is the greatest quality
a man can have.

STAGMANTLE. Sport transcends all national barriers, and it is
some comfort to realize that this tragedy has brought two
great nations closer together.

ISABEL. In the face of this terrible tragedy, one is almost
tempted to believe in the grim old legend of the Demon.

[*A figure having the shape of the* ABBOT, *wearing a
monk's habit and a judge's wig and holding the crystal
in his hands, is illuminated at a somewhat higher level
of the stage.*]

ABBOT. I am truly sorry for this young man, but I must ask
for the Court to be cleared.

[*Exeunt* SHAWCROSS, LAMP *and* GUNN.]
[*A Blues.* MONKS *enter with a stretcher,* JAMES' *body
is carried in slow procession round the stage and away
into the darkness.*]

STAGMANTLE and ISABEL.

> Stop all the clocks, cut off the telephone,
> Prevent the dog from barking with a juicy bone,
> Silence the pianos and with muffled drum
> Bring out the coffin, let the mourners come.
> Let aeroplanes circle moaning overhead
> Scribbling on the sky the message: He is dead.
> Put crêpe bows round the white necks of the public doves.
> Let the traffic policeman wear black cotton gloves.

> Hold up your umbrellas to keep off the rain
> From Doctor Williams while he opens a vein;
> Life, he pronounces, it is finally extinct.
> Sergeant, arrest that man who said he winked!

> Shawcross will say a few words sad and kind
> To the weeping crowds about the Master-Mind,
> While Lamp with a powerful microscope
> Searches their faces for a sign of hope.

> And Gunn, of course, will drive the motor-hearse:
> None could drive it better, most would drive it worse.
> He'll open up the throttle to its fullest power
> And drive him to the grave at ninety miles an hour.

ABBOT. Please be seated, Mr Ransom. I hope everything has been arranged here to your satisfaction?

RANSOM. I didn't do it! I swear I didn't touch him! It wasn't my fault! [*Pointing to* FIGURE.] The Demon gave the sign! The Demon is real!

ABBOT. In that case, we will call the victims of his pride. Call Ian Shawcross!

CHORUS. Ian Shawcross!

[SHAWCROSS *appears. He is bloodstained and pale.*]

RANSOM. I've had about as much of this as I can stand. You've got to tell them! I hate to bother you with this sort of thing.

SHAWCROSS. I'm afraid you haven't succeeded very well.

RANSOM. You mean, you *did* see something? If you hadn't, you mightn't believe me.

SHAWCROSS. Oh, for Christ's sake, shut up! If what you've done amuses you, I'm glad. I'm not very tolerant, I'm afraid.   [*Exit.*]

ABBOT. Call David Gunn!

CHORUS. David Gunn!

> [*Enter* DAVID GUNN, *pale and covered with snow. His face is entirely without features.*]

RANSOM. David, you saw what happened?

GUNN. Didn't I just? You did it beautifully. It was first class!

RANSOM. You sound pleased!

GUNN. Of course I'm pleased! Who wouldn't be!

RANSOM. David, there's something I *must* tell you——

[*Exit* GUNN.]

ABBOT. Call Edward Lamp!

CHORUS. Edward Lamp! Edward Lamp! Edward Lamp!

LAMP'S VOICE [*far away, off*]. I'm all right.

RANSOM [*shouts*]. Teddy, what did *you* see?

LAMP'S VOICE. If I told you, you wouldn't be any the wiser.

RANSOM. You're on their side, too! Is this all your talk of loyalty amounts to?

MRS A. O, what's the use of your pretending
As if Life had a chance of mending?
There will be nothing to remember
But the fortnight in August or early September.

MR A. Home to supper and to bed.
It'll be like this till we are dead.

[DOCTOR *appears.*]

RANSOM. Tom!

DOCTOR. Just tell me what you want me to do.

RANSOM. I can't face it!

DOCTOR. Perhaps you are right. The Demon demands another kind of victim. Ask the crystal.

[*Exit* DOCTOR.]

ABBOT. You wish to appeal to the crystal, Mr Ransom? Do not ask at once, but think it over.

RANSOM. We haven't a moment to lose. I appeal to the crystal.

ABBOT. Very well, since you wish it, I obey you. [*Looks into crystal.*]

[*Music. Duet from stage-boxes, the* A.'s *sing.*]

MRS A. and MR A.
    Make us kind,
    Make us of one mind,
    Make us brave,
    Save, save, save, save.

ABBOT. Mr Ransom, I did you an injustice. I thought I understood your temptation, but I was wrong. The temptation is not the Demon. If there were no Demon, there would be no temptation.

RANSOM. What have I said? I didn't mean it! Forgive me! It was all my fault. F 6 has shown me what I am. I'm a coward and a prig. I withdraw the charge.

ABBOT. Such altruism, Mr Ransom, is uncommon in one of your race. But I am afraid it is too late now. The case is being brought by the Crown. [*Turning to the* FIGURE *on the summit.*] Have you anything to say in your defence? [*Pause.*] You realize the consequences of silence? [*Pause.*] As long as the world endures there must be law and order. [*To* CHORUS.] Gentlemen, consider your verdict.

CHORUS.
    At last the secret is out, as it always must come in the end,
    The delicious story is ripe to tell to the intimate friend;
    Over the tea-cups and in the square the tongue has its desire;
    Still waters run deep, my dear, there's never smoke without fire.

    Behind the corpse in the reservoir, behind the ghost on the links,
    Behind the lady who dances and the man who madly drinks,

Under the look of fatigue, the attack of migraine and the
    sigh
There is always another story, there is more than meets
    the eye.

For the clear voice suddenly singing, high up in the
    convent wall,
The scent of the elder bushes, the sporting prints in the
    hall,
The croquet matches in summer, the handshake, the
    cough, the kiss,
There is always a wicked secret, a private reason for this.

ABBOT. Have you considered your verdict?

RANSOM. Stop!

> [*He rushes up to the summit and places himself in
> front of the* FIGURE, *with his arms outstretched, as if
> to protect it.*]

RANSOM. No one shall ever——! I couldn't bear it! I'll never
    let them! Never!

ABBOT [*to* CHORUS]. Guilty or not guilty?

CHORUS [*all pointing to the* FIGURE]. Guilty!

GENERAL. Die for England!

ISABEL. Honour!

STAGMANTLE. Service!

GENERAL. Duty!

ISABEL. Sacrifice!

ALL. Die for England.

VOICE. Ostnia.

ALL. England. England. England.

MRS A. and MR A. Die for us!

> [*Thunder and the roar of an avalanche are heard. All
> lights are extinguished below; only the* FIGURE *and*
> RANSOM *remain illuminated.* RANSOM *turns to the*
> FIGURE, *whose draperies fall away, revealing* MRS
> RANSOM *as a young mother.*]

RANSOM. Mother!

MOTHER [MRS RANSOM]. My boy! At last!

> [*He falls at her feet with his head in her lap. She strokes his hair.*]

CHORUS. Acts of injustice done
Between the setting and the rising sun
In history lie like bones, each one.

MRS RANSOM. Still the dark forest, quiet the deep,
Softly the clock ticks, baby must sleep!
The Pole Star is shining, bright the Great Bear,
Orion is watching, high up in the air.

CHORUS. Memory sees them down there,
Paces alive beside his fear
That's slow to die and still here.

MRS RANSOM. Reindeer are coming to drive you away
Over the snow on an ebony sleigh,
Over the mountain and over the sea
You shall go happy and handsome and free.

CHORUS. The future, hard to mark,
Of a world turning in the dark
Where ghosts are walking and dogs bark.

MRS RANSOM. Over the green grass pastures there
You shall go hunting the beautiful deer,
You shall pick flowers, the white and the blue,
Shepherds shall flute their sweetest for you.

CHORUS. True, Love finally is great,
Greater than all; but large the hate,
Far larger than Man can ever estimate.

MRS RANSOM. And in the castle tower above,
The princess' cheek burns red for your love,
You shall be king and queen of the land,
Happy for ever, hand in hand.

CHORUS. But between the day and night
The choice is free to all, and light
Falls equally on black and white.

> [*During the first verse of the Chorale which follows, the light fades from the summit, so that the stage is*

96

completely darkened. Then, after a moment, the entire stage is gradually illuminated by the rising sun. The stage is empty, except for the body of RANSOM, *who lies dead on the summit of the mountain.*]

HIDDEN CHORUS. Free now from indignation,
    Immune from all frustration
    He lies in death alone;
    Now he with secret terror
    And every minor error
    Has also made Man's weakness known.

    Whom history has deserted,
    These have their power exerted,
    In one convulsive throe;
    With sudden drowning suction
    Drew him to his destruction.
    [*Cresc.*] But they to dissolution go.

SLOW CURTAIN

ON THE FRONTIER
a melodrama in three acts

To
BENJAMIN BRITTEN

The drums tap out sensational bulletins;
Frantic the efforts of the violins
To drown the song behind the guarded hill:
The dancers do not listen; but they will.

DRAMATIS PERSONÆ

Dr Oliver Thorvald: *lecturer at a Westland university*
Hilda Thorvald: *his wife*
Eric Thorvald: *their son*
Martha Thorvald: *Dr Thorvald's sister*
Colonel Hussek: *late of the Ostnian Army*
Louisa Vrodny: *his daughter*
Anna Vrodny: *her daughter*
Oswald Vrodny: *brother-in-law to Mrs Vrodny*
Valerian: *head of the Westland Steel Trust*
Lessep: *his secretary*
Manners: *his butler*
Stahl: *a director of the Westland Steel Trust*
The Leader: *of Westland*
Storm-Trooper Grimm: *of the Leader's Bodyguard*
A Chorus of Eight: *five men and three women*

NOTES ON THE CHARACTERS

(All the Chorus must be able to sing)

DR THORVALD: Middle-aged, pedantic, would have been a liberal under a democratic régime.

HILDA THORVALD: Good-natured, a bit slatternly. Has been the butterfly type. Hates rows. Wears dressing-jackets, kimonos, arty clothes.

ERIC THORVALD: Untidy, angular. About twenty.

MARTHA THORVALD: Violently repressed, fanatical. Wears glasses. Not to be played too broadly: remember that, beneath her fanaticism, she is an educated, intelligent woman. She is conscious of having a better brain than her sister-in-law.

COLONEL HUSSEK: An old lobster.

MRS VRODNY: Embittered by poverty and household responsibilities; but with considerable reserves of power. The Vrodny-Hussek family has aristocratic traditions.

ANNA VRODNY: Must not be played as a mouse. She has character, but has hardly realized it.

OSWALD VRODNY: A cheerful ne'er-do-well. Might even speak with an Irish accent.

VALERIAN: Tall, suave, courteous, sardonic. Speaks precisely, with a slight foreign accent. About forty-five.

LESSEP: About twenty-seven. Intriguing. Can be spiteful. In dress and manner slightly pansy.

MANNERS: A stage butler.

STAHL: Though, with Valerian, he plays second fiddle, he is a man of considerable presence and power. He is not quite as tall as Valerian, but broader. About fifty-five.

THE LEADER: Try to avoid resemblances to living personages.

The Leader wears a beard. He is about forty-five, anxious and ill. In the first act, he plays very stiffly, like a newsreel photograph of himself. His platform voice is like a trance-voice, loud and unnatural. He wears uniform throughout.

GRIMM: About twenty-five. Pale and tense. Wears uniform throughout.

TIME: THE PRESENT

ACT ONE: EARLY SUMMER

ACT TWO: A WEEK LATER

ACT THREE: NINE MONTHS LATER

ACT I

(*BEFORE THE CURTAIN*)

[*Slow music. Eight workers—three women and five men—are grouped as if waiting for the gates of a factory to open. They sing in turn the following couplets:*]

The clock on the wall gives an electric tick,
I'm feeling sick, brother; I'm feeling sick.

The sirens blow at eight; the sirens blow at noon;
Goodbye, sister, goodbye; we shall die soon.

Mr Valerian has a mansion on the hill;
It's a long way to the grave, brother; a long way still.

The assembly-belt is like an army on the move;
It's stronger than hate, brother; it's stronger than love.

The major came down with a pipe in his face;
Work faster, sister, faster, or you'll lose your place.

The major wears pointed shoes, and calls himself a gent;
I'm behind with the rent, brother; I'm behind with the rent.

The missus came in with her hair down, a-crying:
'Stay at home, George, stay at home, for baby's dying!'

There's grit in my lungs, there's sweat on my brow;
You were pretty once, Lisa, but oh, just look at you now!

You looked so handsome in your overalls of blue;
It was summer, Johnny, and I never knew.

My mother told me, when I was still a lad:
'Johnny, leave the girls alone.' I wish I had.

The lathe on number five has got no safety-guard.
It's hard to lose your fingers, sister, mighty hard.

Went last night to the pictures; the girl was almost bare,
The boy spent a million dollars on that love-affair.

[*The factory siren sounds. The workers begin to move across the stage and exit L. The last verses are punctuated by the sound of clocking-in.*]

When the hammer falls, the sparks fly up like stars;
If I were rich, brother, I'd have ten motor-cars.

Pass the word, sister, pass it along the line:
There's a meeting tonight at number forty-nine.

Oil that bearing, watch that dynamo;
When it's time to strike, brother, I'll let you know.

Stoke up the fires in furnace number three;
The day is coming, brother, when we shall all be free!

ACT I

SCENE I

[VALERIAN'S *study.* VALERIAN'S *house is supposed to stand on high ground, overlooking the capital city of Westland. At the back of the stage there is a deep bay-window. The furniture is chiefly modern, but there are a number of statuettes and valuable etchings. A desk with telephones. A radiogram. Doors L. and R.*]

> [*When the curtain rises,* MANNERS *is arranging the chair-cushions, while* LESSEP *puts papers in order on the desk. It is a fine morning in early summer.*]

LESSEP. Oh, by the way, Manners . . . your Master will be lunching on the terrace, this morning.

MANNERS. Indeed, Sir? Are those Mr Valerian's orders, Sir?

LESSEP [*sharply*]. Of course they're Mr Valerian's orders. What did you suppose?

MANNERS. I beg your pardon, Sir. I mention it only because Mr Valerian has been accustomed to leave the management of this household entirely in *my* hands. This is the first time, in twelve years, that he has thought it necessary to say where he wished to lunch.

LESSEP. Well, it won't be the last time, I can assure you!

MANNERS. No, Sir?

LESSEP. No!

[*Enter* VALERIAN, *L.*]

VALERIAN. Good morning, Lessep.

LESSEP. Good morning, Mr Valerian.

VALERIAN. Are those ready for me to sign? [*Sees* MANNERS *is waiting.*] Yes, what is it?

MANNERS. Excuse me, Sir. Am I to take it that you ordered lunch to be served on the terrace?

113

VALERIAN. Since when, Manners, have I given you orders about my meals? I am the master of this house, not the mistress.

MANNERS. Exactly, Sir. Today I had thought of serving lunch in the Winter Garden. The terrace, in my humble opinion, would be too hot in this weather. The Leader, I am given to understand, dislikes the heat. But Mr Lessep said——

VALERIAN. Mr Lessep was mistaken. We bow to your judgment, Manners. The Winter Garden.

MANNERS. Thank you, Sir.

[*Bows and exit, R.*]

LESSEP. Mr Valerian . . . I hope you'll forgive me. . . .

VALERIAN. I can forgive anything, Lessep—except incompetence. Just now you behaved officiously, and tactlessly. Never mind. I am quite fairly satisfied with you, at present. As long as you continue to be competent, I shall not have to bother the Ostnians for another secretary. . . .

LESSEP [*staggered*]. I . . . I don't think I quite understand. . . .

VALERIAN. No? Then I will speak more plainly. You are in the employ of the Ostnian Steel Combine. . . . Oh, pray don't suppose that you are the first! Despite the general identity of our interests, it is a regrettable fact that the Ostnian industrialists do not trust us—and that we, I am sorry to say, do not entirely trust the Ostnians. So we both prefer to rely on inside information. . . . It is an arrangement which suits me very well. All I ask is that the employees the Ostnians send us (always by the most devious routes) shall be efficient. We also have sent them some admirable secretaries. . . . Now, do we understand each other?

LESSEP. Mr Valerian, on my word of honour——

VALERIAN [*signing papers*]. Very well. I have no time for arguments. I am not asking for a confession. . . . Oh, one more little point: yesterday, you took from my safe the plans of the new Valerian tank and photographed them. Clumsily. You are not accustomed to this kind of work, I think? It requires practice.

LESSEP. I'm ready to swear that I never touched——

VALERIAN [*still writing*]. Yes, yes. Of course. . . . But in order that you shall not commit a gaffe which might seriously prejudice your prospects with your employers, let me tell you that we have already sold this tank to the Ostnian War Office. . . . You didn't know? Too stupid, isn't it? Lack of departmental co-operation, as always. It will be the ruin of both our countries. . . .

LESSEP [*collapsing*]. I'd better leave at once. . . .

VALERIAN. Nonsense! You will learn. . . . No tears, I beg! They bore me indescribably. . . . We have wasted four minutes on an exceedingly dull subject. . . . And now tell me, please: what are my appointments for today?

LESSEP [*pulling himself together with an effort*]. Mr Stahl is coming in to see you at twelve-thirty. He will remain to meet the Leader, at lunch. This afternoon you will accompany the Leader on his inspection of the Works. And you wanted, if possible, to get away in time for the Poussin auction, at four forty-five. . . .

VALERIAN. Ah, to be sure—the Poussins! The one bright moment of a dreary day! I mustn't miss them on any account. And the Leader will speak for an hour, at least. . . . Please arrange an interruption. At the first opportunity, our operatives are to burst spontaneously into the National Hymn. Spontaneously, mind you. . . . It's the only known method of cutting short the Leader's flow of imperatives.

LESSEP. I'll see to it, Mr Valerian.

VALERIAN. You'd better go down there now, and talk to some of our foremen. They're accustomed to organize these things.

LESSEP. Is there anything else?

VALERIAN. Nothing, thank you.

LESSEP [*prepares to go, hesitates*]. Mr Valerian—I just want to say: I shall never forget your generosity. . . .

VALERIAN. My dear boy, I am never generous—as you will very soon discover to your cost. Please do not flatter yourself that your conscience and its scruples interest me in the very slightest degree. In this establishment, there is no joy over the sinner that repents. . . . Very well. You may go.

[*Exit* LESSEP, R. VALERIAN *goes thoughtfully upstage to the window, and stands looking out over the city.*]

VALERIAN. The Valerian Works. . . . How beautiful they look from here! Much nicer than the cathedral next door. . . . A few people still go there to pray, I suppose—peasants who have only been in the city a generation, middle-class women who can't get husbands. . . . Curious to think that it was once the centre of popular life. If I had been born in the thirteenth century, I suppose I should have wanted to be a bishop. [*Factory sirens, off, sound the lunch-hour.*] Now my sirens have supplanted his bells. But the crowd down there haven't changed much. The Dole is as terrifying as Hell-Fire—probably worse. . . . Run along, little man. Lunch is ready for you in the Valerian Cafeteria. Why so anxious? You shall have every care. You may spoon in the Valerian Park, and buy the ring next day at the Valerian Store. Then you shall settle down in a cosy Valerian villa, which, I assure you, has been highly praised by architectural experts. The Valerian School, equipped with the very latest apparatus, will educate your dear little kiddies in Patriotism and Personal Hygiene. A smart Valerian Family Runabout will take you on Sundays to picnic by the waterfall, along with several hundred others of your kind. The Valerian Bank will look after your savings, if any; our doctors will see to your health, and our funeral parlours will bury you. . . . And then you talk about Socialism! Oh yes, I am well aware that university professors, who ought to know better, have assured you that you are the heir to all the ages. Nature's last and most daring experiment. Believe them, by all means, if it helps you to forget the whip. Indulge in all the longings that aspirin and sweet tea and stump oratory can arouse. Dream of your never-never land, where the parks are covered with naked cow-like women, quite free; where the rich are cooked over a slow fire, and pigeons coo from the cupolas. Let the band in my park convince you that Life is seriously interested in marital fidelity and the right

116

use of leisure, in the reign of happiness and peace. Go on, go on. Think what you like, vote for whom you like. What difference does it make? Make your little protest. Get a new master if you can. You will soon be made to realize that he is as exacting as the old, and probably less intelligent. . . . The truth is, Nature is not interested in underlings— in the lazy, the inefficient, the self-indulgent, the People. Nor, for that matter, in the Aristocracy, which is now only another name for the Idle Rich. The idle are never powerful. With their gigolos and quack doctors, they are as unhappy as the working classes who can afford neither, and a great deal more bored. The world has never been governed by the People or by the merely Rich, and it never will be. It is governed by men like myself—though, in practice, we are usually rich and often come from the People.

[*He moves away from the window to the desk and picks up a signed photograph of the Leader.*]

No, not by you, dear Leader. You're one of the People, really, which is why they love you, you poor muddle-headed bundle of nerves, so overworked and so hypno-tized by the sound of your own voice that you will never know what's happening nor who pulls the strings. Do you think, my modern Caesar, that the Roman emperors were important? They weren't. It was the Greek freedmen, who kept the accounts, who mattered. The cardinals mattered in the Middle Ages, not those dreary feudal barons.

[*He picks up a statuette.*]

No, perhaps that's wrong, too. Real political power is only made possible by electricity, double entry and high explosives. Perhaps, after all, the hermits and the artists were wiser. Nothing is worth while except complete mastery, and, in those days, that could only be achieved over the Self. I wonder what it felt like to be St Francis Stylites or Poussin. Well, times have changed. The arts haven't been important since the eighteenth century.

Today, a creative man becomes an engineer or a scientist, not an artist. He leaves that career to neurotics and humbugs who can't succeed at anything else. [*Back at the window.*] This is probably the last period of human history. The political régimes of the future may have many fancy names, but never again will the common man be allowed to rule his own life or judge for himself. To be an artist or a saint has ceased to be modern. . . . Yes, for the man of power, there can now be but one aim—absolute control of mankind.

[*Enter* MANNERS, R.]

MANNERS. Mr Stahl, Sir.

[*Enter* STAHL, R.]

VALERIAN. Ah, my dear Stahl, welcome home! [*Exit* MANNERS, R.]

STAHL. How are you, Valerian? You're looking well. [*Looks round the room.*] It seems strange to be in this room again. . . . You've bought a new etching, I see?

VALERIAN. Oh, I have a great deal to show you. But that can wait. You had a pleasant journey, I hope?

STAHL. Thanks, yes. Excellent.

VALERIAN. You only got back yesterday morning?

STAHL. And I've been run off my feet ever since!

VALERIAN. Your wife is well, I trust?

STAHL. Not as well as I should like. She's been suffering a lot with her migraine, lately. Extraordinary thing, migraine. Nobody really understands it. She stayed on in Paris to see that new Swedish man; he's discovered a special injection. I hope it'll do her some good.

VALERIAN. I am truly sorry to hear this. . . . And your boy? I hope his studies are progressing favourably?

STAHL. Well . . . yes and no. Igor works hard enough, but he's so undecided. He wants to give up engineering and read Icelandic. . . . I suppose it's just a phase. . . .

VALERIAN. My dear Stahl, you are indeed the model family man! Your worries never cease!

118

STAHL. Upon my word, Valerian, I sometimes envy you. When one sees you in this charming house, surrounded by your treasures, with no wife to run up milliner's bills! The world looks black enough, these days, Heaven knows—but at least a bachelor has only himself to think of. . . .

VALERIAN. Always the pessimist! Which reminds me that I haven't yet thanked you for all those admirably lucid and exceedingly depressing letters. . . .

STAHL. Well, I'm glad, at any rate, that you found them lucid!

VALERIAN. So much so that, as soon as I heard you were returning, I arranged for the Leader to come and hear the worst from Cassandra's own lips. There is nothing he so much enjoys as bad news—about foreign countries: England doomed, Germany bankrupt, the United States heading for her last and greatest slump. . . . Mind you lay it on thick! And with particular emphasis on the contrast between decadent, anarchical Ostnia and our own dear Westland—that paradise of solvency and order.

STAHL. I only hope the food won't choke me as I say it!

VALERIAN. My dear friend, you can have confidence in my chef: Ananias himself could lunch here with perfect impunity. . . . Though really it's a wonder I wasn't suffocated myself, the other evening: I had to spend an hour praising the works of the new National Academy of Art—Putensen, de Kloot, and those exquisite little landscapes (or should I say 'cowscapes'?) of Ketchling. . . .

STAHL. Ketchling? But surely he's the man who does the hair-tonic advertisements?

VALERIAN. What a memory you have! A rather dangerous memory, if I may say so, for these times. . . . Yes, it all happened about three months ago. You were in Brazil, I believe? Poor Milnik was so unfortunate as to offend the Minister of Propaganda. Next morning, he was discovered to possess an Ostnian great-grandmother, and, within a week, Ketchling had stepped into his shoes. . . . Ketchling's wife, I may add, had been having an affair with our respected Postmaster-General. . . .

STAHL. The Postmaster? But surely Madame Korteniz . . . .

VALERIAN. The reign of Madame Korteniz has ended, quite suddenly, under rather amusing circumstances. . . . But that's a long story, which will keep. Here I am, gossiping away like an old concierge, and you have told me nothing about your journey! First of all, how does Westland appear to a returned traveller—sadly provincial, I fear? There have been changes since you left, and none of them for the better. Since the Leader's newest statue was unveiled, it has become necessary to walk down Victory Avenue with one's eyes tightly closed. I always tell my chauffeur to make a detour. . . .

STAHL. Yes, I've seen that monstrosity already. . . . But I'm sorry to say that, since my return, I've received even worse shocks——

VALERIAN. Ah, you mean the neo-Egyptian portico of the new Culture House? Well, it's a nice point. The Leader, you'll admit, is the uglier of the two; but the Culture House is so much larger. . . .

STAHL. There's more wrong with this country than its architecture, Valerian. You know that better than I do. Coming back like this, after six months, one's appalled, simply appalled by the way things are going. Of course, I haven't had time to make detailed enquiries, yet; but I talked to the works managers early this morning, and yesterday I was at the Stock Exchange and around the clubs. People are afraid to say much, naturally; but I drew my own conclusions.

VALERIAN. Which were, no doubt, as gloomy as usual? I shall listen to them with the greatest interest. But not, my dear Stahl, *not* before lunch! You will ruin both our appetites.

STAHL. I know that it amuses you to be flippant. But these are facts. You can't pass them by, like the Leader's statue, with your eyes shut. . . . Something must be done, and done quickly. We're in for really big trouble. Conditions at the labour camps are getting worse all the time. The men are complaining quite openly: six months ago, they wouldn't have dared. The food isn't fit for an African village. The buildings leak—what can you expect from that Army

120

contract stuff? T.B. is definitely on the increase. As for the Shock Troops—if even fifty per cent of what I hear is true—the whole organization's rotten from top to bottom; and the commandants are responsible only to the Leader —which means to nobody at all. If you want to see them on business, you must search the night-clubs and the brothels; they never go near their offices. At the barracks, you'll hear the same story: the Leader has broken every promise he ever made. The same thing down at the Works. Agitators have been getting at the men, secret unions are being formed. I even heard rumours of a stay-in strike. . . .

VALERIAN. My dear friend, your sojourn in the democratic countries seems to have confused your ideas, a little! Surely you are aware that here, in our happy Westland, the Leader has declared all strikes illegal?

STAHL. An illegal strike is simply an insurrection.

VALERIAN. Which can be dealt with as such.

STAHL. Which *cannot* be dealt with! You know as well as I do that the troops would refuse to fire. Why, the General Staff wouldn't even dare to give the order!

VALERIAN. Aren't we becoming rather melodramatic? Do you, seriously, in your heart of hearts, believe that things could ever come to shooting? In Russia, yes. In Spain, yes. Never in Westland. You know our countrymen; a nation of grumblers—and grumblers are never dangerous. The situation is bad, of course—disgraceful, appalling, but hardly serious. When you have been at home a week or two, you will recapture that peculiar Westland sense of proportion—as lop-sided as Putensen's nudes—and you will agree with me.

STAHL. Perhaps I shall. Yes . . . that's just what I'm afraid of. . . . But now, before I begin to squint like the rest of you, let me tell you that, in my considered opinion, this country is on the verge of a revolution!

VALERIAN. Revolution! Revolution! Eternally that bogey word! When the old Emperor abdicated, everybody predicted a revolution, and what did we get? A cabinet of shop-keepers in ill-fitting top hats, who misquoted Marx and scrambled to cultivate the society of effete aristocrats, whose titles they themselves had just abolished by decree. The workers were impressed by their socialist speeches, and tried to act upon them—so the shopkeeper-marxists called them bolsheviks and traitors, dissolved parliament, suppressed the unions and established a dictatorship which lacked nothing but a dictator. Then came the Leader, in his fancy-dress uniform, and these same shopkeepers rejoiced, because the National Revolution was to make an end of the Valerian Works, and all the big business concerns and open the garden of paradise to the small trader. And what did the Leader do? Crying: 'Revolution!' he obligingly ruined a number of our lesser competitors and business rivals. He did not dare to touch the Valerian Trust. He did not want to touch it. Without us, he could not exist for a fortnight. . . . As for the workers, who you so much dread—they play at secret meetings, of which I am informed, and at printing illegal pamphlets, which litter my desk at this moment. The workers are all patient sheep, or silly crowing cockerels, or cowardly rabbits. . . .

[*Enter* MANNERS, *R.*]

MANNERS. I beg your pardon, Sir. The Leader's Bodyguard has arrived. They wish to make the—ah, usual inspection.

STAHL. Good Heavens! Whatever for?

VALERIAN. Oh, you will soon get used to these little formalities. A month ago, there was another attempt on the Leader's life. Hushed up, naturally. But I thought the foreign press would have got hold of it? Since then, precautions have been doubled. The Leader never visits a strange house without assuring himself that there are no assassins hiding on the premises. . . . Very well. Let one of them come in.

[MANNERS *exits for a moment and re-enters with Storm-Trooper,* GRIMM.]

GRIMM [*giving Westland Salute*]. For Westland. . . . I have orders to search this floor.

122

VALERIAN. By all means. Please make yourself quite at home.

GRIMM [*indicating door, L.*]. Where does that door lead to?

VALERIAN. To my bedroom, my bathroom, and the back staircase. . . . But, surely, you've been here before?

GRIMM. I only joined the Bodyguard last week.

VALERIAN. I see. . . . Strange. I seem to remember your face.

GRIMM [*quickly*]. That's impossible. I come from the eastern province.

VALERIAN. Well, we all make mistakes. . . . Pray don't let me detain you from your duties. And don't forget to look under the bed.

[GRIMM *salutes and exit, L.*]

VALERIAN [*to* MANNERS]. You'd better go with him, I think. He might take a fancy to my silver hair-brushes.

[MANNERS *bows and exit, L.*]

VALERIAN. There goes one of the rulers of our country!

STAHL. Common gangsters!

VALERIAN. After all, there is a good deal to be said for gangsters. One's dealings with them are so charmingly simple. They understand two things: money and the whip. They know where their bread and butter comes from. The Leader is much safer with these boys than with a pack of crooked politicians.

STAHL. By the way, how is the Leader, nowadays? In Paris, there was a lot of talk about his—health.

VALERIAN. With good reason, I'm afraid. You know, three weeks ago, he had a very serious breakdown. I'm told Pegoud was sent for. . . .

STAHL. Whew! So he's really mad, at last!

VALERIAN. My dear friend, the Leader has always been mad. The really alarming symptom is that he's beginning to recover. The crises are becoming isolated, less predictable, much more violent. He is no longer the roaring waterfall, whose power could be utilized and whose noise was harmless. He is the volcano which may suddenly destroy cities

123

and men. . . . I ought to warn you: if any little disturbance occurs during lunch, please appear to take no notice. And, when it is over, behave as if nothing had happened. . . .

STAHL. A nice party you've let me in for, I must say! I'm beginning to feel quite scared. . . . I've only spoken to the Leader twice in my life. I'd no idea you knew him so intimately.

VALERIAN. I've been seeing a good deal of him, lately. He interests me. I have been studying, as the Americans say, the secret of his success.

STAHL. And what is this secret?

VALERIAN. The Leader, you see, is our national martyr. We Westlanders are a stolid, insensitive race: we need someone to do our suffering for us. The Leader bears upon his shoulders all the wrongs, all the griefs that Westland ever suffered—and many more besides. When the fat placid housewives attend his meetings, and see him rave and wring his hands, and tremble and weep, they shake their heads in their motherly way, and murmur: 'Poor Leader —he is going through all this for *us*!' Then they return to their tea, with whipped cream and apple cakes, purged and ennobled, by proxy.

STAHL. But what beats me is how one can have any kind of personal relationship with him. Why, he isn't a man at all! He's a gramophone!

VALERIAN. No doubt. But even a gramophone can be made to play better and more harmonious records. . . . As a matter of fact, your mentioning gramophones was unintentionally apt. The Leader often drops in to listen to mine.

STAHL. You mean to say that you actually *play* to him!

VALERIAN. Oh yes, indeed. Like Orpheus. Whenever he seems tired and dispirited, or the conversation flags. . . . I flatter myself that I am educating him, slowly but surely. . . . We started with *Narcissus* and the *Melody in F*. After a fortnight, he was getting tired of them, so I prescribed *The War March of the Priests*—all too successfully. I think even Mendelssohn himself would have wished he had never written it. . . . At length, we passed on to the *Pathetic*

124

Symphony, and, I am happy to say, outgrew it at the end of a weary month. At present, Rameau's *Tambourin* is the favourite. It seems likely to last through the summer. . . .

STAHL. Really, Valerian, you've missed your vocation! You should have been a lion-tamer!

[*Enter* MANNERS, *R.*]

MANNERS. The Leader has arrived, Sir.

STAHL. Good Gracious! He nearly caught us talking high treason!

[*Noises off. Someone shouts: 'Guard! Attention!' The Leader's voice is heard, saying: 'For Westland!' Enter* THE LEADER, *R.* MANNERS *exits, R., behind him.*]

LEADER [*salutes*]. For Westland! [*Shakes hands.*] How are you, Valerian?

VALERIAN. Delighted to see you, Sir. . . . I believe you know Mr Stahl, one of our directors?

STAHL. You will hardly remember me, my Leader. We met last at the Industrial Banquet.

LEADER. I never forget a face. [*Salutes.*] For Westland!

VALERIAN. I hope we see you in good health?

[*Enter* MANNERS, *with cocktails, R.*]

LEADER. My health is at the service of my country. Therefore it is good.

[MANNERS *hands round cocktails and exit, R.*]

VALERIAN. May it long continue so! Mr Stahl, as I told you in my letter, has just returned from a business tour of Europe and America. I wanted you to hear his impressions.

STAHL. There are certain points which might possibly interest you, my Leader.

LEADER. Everything interests me. When I study any subject, I acquaint myself with its smallest details. [*Raising his glass.*] Westland!

VALERIAN ⎫
STAHL   ⎬ [*both drinking*]. Westland!

LEADER [*to* STAHL]. Tell me, is it true that, in London, negroes are even permitted to play in the dance orchestras?

STAHL. Well—yes, certainly.

LEADER. I was right! Only a dying race could show such tolerance. England is becoming a foreign colony. Very soon, they'll be having Ostnians in to drive the trams! Ha, ha, ha!

[VALERIAN *and* STAHL *laugh dutifully.*]

[*Enter* MANNERS, *R.*]

MANNERS. Lunch is served, Sir.

[*Exit, R.*]

LEADER. I am in good spirits, today! What beautiful weather! We shall have a real Westland summer! Valerian, I have a surprise for you. After inspecting your Works, I shall take you for a drive in the park.

VALERIAN [*suppressing a groan*]. That will be delightful! Shall we go downstairs?

LEADER [*ignoring him*]. I want to have young faces around me —youth, health, springtime. The perfume of the flowers. The smell of the trees. The lithe active bodies of our splendid Westland children. . . . Ah, it does one good!

VALERIAN. I can imagine no more charming way of spending the afternoon. . . . Perhaps you'd like to have lunch? Then we can start earlier on our programme. . . .

LEADER [*as before*]. I was thinking, too, that we might visit your model cottages. I am never so happy as when I can spare a few moments from my work to spend among the common people. How delighted and surprised they will be to have their Leader among them! I love to watch their contented smiles as they bend over their humble tasks, working proudly, for Westland, each in his own sphere. How well I understand them! How well I know their wants! I know what they are thinking even before they know it themselves. It is my mission to restore to every Westlander the dignity of labour, to put good honest tools into his hands, to guard him from crafty, underhand

126

foreign competition. Westland must awake! Westland must throw off her fetters! Westland must raise the heavy load of poverty from the shoulders of the groaning poor. [*He picks up a paper-weight from the desk.*] Westland must——

VALERIAN [*tactfully taking the paper-weight from the Leader's hand*]. Bravo, Sir! Bravo! I hope you'll say that to our operatives, this afternoon. It will inspire them. . . . Lunch is ready. Shall we go down?

LEADER [*suddenly cut short in the middle of his enthusiasm, stares stupidly, for a moment, at his empty hand. Then, as if coming to earth, he says quietly*]. Ah, yes—lunch. . . .

CURTAIN

(*BEFORE THE CURTAIN*)

[*A ray of light, barred with shadow, as if through a prison window, illuminates four prisoners, two women and two men. They are squatting on the ground, handcuffed. Their faces are ghastly.*]

[*Air: 'Sweet Betsy from Pike'.*]

FIRST PRISONER [*sings*].

    Industrialists, bankers, in comfortable chairs
    Are saying: 'We still have control of affairs.
    The Leader will have all our enemies shot.'

ALL. They would like to forget us, but, O, they cannot!

SECOND PRISONER.

    The idle, the rich, and the shabby genteel
    And the clever who think that the world isn't real
    Say: 'The forces of order have triumphed! We're safe!'

ALL. But the world has its own views on how to behave!

THIRD PRISONER.

    The judge sits on high in a very fine wig,
    He talks about Law and he talks very big,
    And chaplains in church say: 'Obedience is best.'

ALL. We've heard that before and we're not much impressed!

FOURTH PRISONER.

    The Leader stands up on his platform and shouts:
    'Follow me and you never need have any doubts!
    Put on my uniform, wave my great flag!'

ALL. But when the wind blows he shall burst like a bag!

FIRST PRISONER.

    'If you're foolish enough,' they declare, 'to resist,
    You shall feel the full weight of fieldboot and fist.'
    They beat us with truncheons, they cast us in jail,

ALL. But all their forms of persuasion shall fail!

SECOND PRISONER.

    They boast: 'We shall last for a thousand long years,'
    But History, it happens, has other ideas.
    'We shall live on for ever!' they cry, but instead

ALL. They shall die soon defending the cause of the dead!
THIRD PRISONER.

> They talk of the mystical value of Blood,
> Of War as a holy and purifying flood,
> Of bullets and bombs as the true works of art.

ALL. They'll change their opinion when shot through the heart!
FOURTH PRISONER.

> Perhaps we shall die by a firing-squad,
> Perhaps they will kill us, that wouldn't be odd,
> But when we lie down with the earth on our face

ALL. There'll be ten more much better to fight in our place!
ALL. The night may seem lonely, the night may seem long,

> But Time is patient and that's where they're wrong!
> For Truth shall flower and Error explode
> And the people be free then to choose their own road!

BLACK OUT

ACT I

SCENE II

[*The Ostnia-Westland Room. It is not to be supposed that the Frontier between the two countries does actually pass through this room: the scene is only intended to convey the idea of the Frontier—the L. half of the stage being in Westland: the R. half being in Ostnia. The furnishing of the two halves should suggest differences in national characteristics, and also in the nature of the two families which inhabit them: the Thorvalds' (Westland) home is academic; the Vrodny-Hussek (Ostnian) home is comfortable, reactionary, bourgeois. Each home has a door and window, L. and R. respectively. On the back wall of each hangs a big portrait, with a wireless-set standing beneath it. The Thorvalds have a portrait of the Westland 'Leader', who is bearded and ferocious-looking: the Vrodny-Hussek family have a portrait of the King of Ostnia, very suave and gracious, with orders and much gold braid. The chairs are arranged in two semicircles, and the concentration of lighting should heighten the impression of an invisible barrier between the two halves of the stage. The two groups of characters (with the exceptions to be noted later) seem absolutely unaware of each other's existence.*]

[*It is evening. When the curtain rises, DR OLIVER THORVALD, the University professor, is writing at his desk. MRS THORVALD is laying cards at a table, and ERIC their son, who is a student, sits writing in an armchair with a book-rest.*]

[*On the other side of the stage, MRS VRODNY is darning socks, seated on the sofa. Her father, COLONEL HUSSEK, sits reading the newspaper in an invalid wheel-chair.*]

DR THORVALD [*pausing to read aloud what he has written*].
'Professor Jongden appears to have modelled his style

upon the more sensational articles in the popular press of his country. For his scholarship, however, we can discover no precedent. His emendations would not convince a commercial traveller. The authorities he quotes, and as frequently misquotes, are most of them out of date. Beyer's great work on the Ionian Laws he does not so much as mention; no doubt he is unwilling to acknowledge that any contribution to culture could be made by a nation which he has always been taught to regard as barbarian.'

COL. HUSSEK [*reading from newspaper*]. 'The Minister for Propaganda has banned the sale in Ostnia of the Westland *Sunday Sun* for one month—as the result of the insulting caricatures of His Majesty, published in last Sunday's issue. . . .' I can't think what the country's coming to! Thirty years ago, they wouldn't have dared! The old King must turn in his grave. He would never have allowed our honour to be——

MRS VRODNY [*bitterly*]. Nobody cares about honour, these days! All they think of now is Self!

COL. HUSSEK. You're right, Louisa! Our young people have no sense of Ostnian loyalty.

MRS VRODNY. You've no idea, Father, how rude the shopgirls are, nowadays! I could smack their faces sometimes; they're so insolent. And the prices! Mother would have had a fit! [*Holds up a sock with an enormous hole in it.*] Just look at that! How Oswald manages to wear his socks into such holes I can't imagine!

DR THORVALD [*reading aloud*]. 'We strongly advise the Professor to leave the classics alone and to betake himself to a sphere to which his talents are less unfitted. We suggest that the scandals of the Ostnian Court would be a suitable choice.'

ERIC. Who are you attacking this time, Father?

DR THORVALD. Jongden has just brought out a book on Ionia —a typical Ostnian piece of work. All superficial brilliance and fluff, with nothing behind it. No Ostnian ever made a scholar. They think it vulgar to take trouble.

ERIC. But isn't he the man who's been offered a chair at Yale?

DR THORVALD. Just because he can make amusing little speeches after dinner, they prefer him to a real scholar, like Beyer! It's preposterous! He can't hold a candle to him!

MRS THORVALD. You know, dear, it's only because Beyer is a Westlander. And they believe all the lies their newspapers spread about us. I can't understand why they're allowed to print such stuff. The Leader ought to put a stop to it.

COL. HUSSEK. Tcha! Another lightning strike at the Docks! If they'd only shoot a few of them, it'd put a stop to all this nonsense!

MRS VRODNY. I'm sure it's only due to Westland agitators, Father. The Ostnian working-man would never behave like that of his own accord. He's got too much commonsense. He knows it only puts up the cost of living.

MRS THORVALD. The Ace of Diamonds. . . . Do you think that means I've won a prize in the *Sunday Sun* Doublets, or only that Martha's ordered enough vegetables to go round? She so seldom does. . . . Eric dear, I do wish you wouldn't work so hard! I'm sure it can't be good for you. Why don't you go out and do field-exercises, like the other students?

DR THORVALD. Leave the boy alone, Hilda. You can't become a scholar without keeping your nose to the grindstone, eh Eric? [*Rises from desk and comes over to* ERIC'S *chair lighting his pipe.*] What are you writing on, this time? [*Looks over* ERIC'S *shoulder.*] 'The chances of European peace'! What a ridiculous subject! Surely Professor Bluteisen never set you that?

ERIC. No. I'm doing it for a few of my friends. Some of us are trying to think these things out.

DR THORVALD. You're wasting your time, my boy. What chances are there of peace—with the Ostnians arming to the teeth? I tell you, Europe's a powder-magazine. It only needs a spark.

MRS THORVALD. Martha says the war's coming this year. It's all in Revelations, she says. She tried to explain it to me, but she's so difficult to understand: her false teeth fit so badly.

ERIC. Don't talk like that, Mother! Of course there'll be a war if we all go on saying and thinking there will be, and doing nothing to stop it. Why are we all so frightened? None of us *want* war.

MRS THORVALD. *We* don't, but what about the Ostnians?

COL. HUSSEK. Notes. Negotiations. . . . We're too polite to them; that's our trouble!

MRS VRODNY. The Westlander's a bully. Always has been.

DR THORVALD. After the last war, when we were weak, they bullied us. And it's only now, when the Leader's shown them that Westland won't stand any nonsense, that they've learnt to mind their p's and q's a bit.

COL. HUSSEK. The only thing the Westlander understands is the stick. We ought to have finished the job properly, last time.

ERIC. How do you know the Ostnians want war?

MRS THORVALD. Haven't they always hated us? Haven't they always been jealous of us? Especially since our national revolution.

DR THORVALD. They're jealous of our liberty and power of creative progress.

MRS VRODNY. The trouble is, they've no traditions. That's why they're jealous of us. They always have been. They're spoilt children, really.

DR THORVALD. A decadent race is always jealous of a progressive one.

MRS VRODNY. You may say what you like; tradition and breeding count.

MRS THORVALD. You may say what you like, Eric. You can't wipe out the history of a thousand years.

COL. HUSSEK. Damned bolsheviks!

ERIC. Well, I think that if people—the ordinary decent people in both countries—would only get together, we could . . .

[*Enter* ANNA VRODNY, *R*., *with a shopping basket. The effect of her presence upon* ERIC *is instantly noticeable.*

133

He breaks off in the middle of his sentence, as though he had forgotten what it was he had meant to say. Throughout the rest of the scene he follows ANNA's *movements eagerly with his eyes.* ANNA, *also, is watching* ERIC, *but more timidly and covertly. Nobody else on the stage appears to notice this.*]

MRS VRODNY. Oh, there you are a last, Anna! Whatever have you been doing all this time?

DR THORVALD. Could what, Eric?

ANNA. I'm sorry, Mother. There was such a queue at Benets'.

[*Begins to take parcels out of basket and lay them on the table.*]

DR THORVALD. Well, go on! What could you do?

MRS THORVALD. Oh, don't argue so, Oliver! It makes my head ache!

DR THORVALD. Sorry, my dear. I was only trying to make him see how woolly-minded he is. And Westland has no use for woolliness, these days. I've got to go now to a meeting of the tutorial board, to consider the case of those so-called pacifist demonstrators yesterday. And I don't mind telling you, Eric, that I shall vote for their expulsion from the University. Let that be a warning to you, my boy!

[*Exit* DR THORVALD, *L.*]

MRS VRODNY [*rising from the sofa to inspect* ANNA's *purchases*]. You call that a chicken? Why didn't you go to Litvaks?

ANNA. But, Mother, you said Litvaks was so expensive!

MRS VRODNY. Oh, it's hopeless! I can't trust any of you to do the simplest things! I work my fingers to the bone for you all, and nobody helps me in the least!

MRS THORVALD. The Queen of Hearts! Well I never! At my age! It must be for you, Eric! How exciting!

MRS VRODNY. Don't stand there dawdling, Anna! We've got to get supper ready. It'll be late as it is.

[MRS VRODNY *and* ANNA *collect the parcels and exeunt, R. During the scene which follows,* COL. HUSSEK *falls gradually asleep.*]

134

MRS THORVALD. The cards never lie! Eric, I don't believe
you're listening!

ERIC. Sorry, Mother, I was just thinking about something.

[*Enter L.* MARTHA THORVALD, *Dr Thorvald's sister,
with a prayer-book and a bunch of flowers. She pauses
solemnly, before speaking, to salute the Leader's
portrait.*]

MARTHA. Cards again? Really, Hilda, I'm surprised at you,
indulging in that sinful nonsense!

MRS THORVALD. Oh, Martha! It isn't nonsense!

MARTHA [*arranging flowers in a vase before the* LEADER'S
portrait]. It's wicked superstition. . . . There! Don't these
look beautiful, under the Leader's picture? They're just
the colour of his eyes! Pastor Brock preached a wonderful
sermon about him today. . . .

MRS THORVALD. The Pastor's such a fine man, but I do wish
he wouldn't shout so. He makes my head ache.

MARTHA. Westland needs more like him! He took as his text:
'I come not to bring peace, but a sword!'

ERIC. Pastor Brock isn't a Christian at all. He wants to rewrite
the Bible.

MARTHA. Eric! How dare you!

ERIC. 'They that live by the sword shall perish by the sword.'
How does he explain that?

MARTHA. I suppose you think you're clever: sitting there and
sneering, while every decent young Westlander is out
learning to defend his country? If I were your Mother——

MRS THORVALD. Oh, my poor head! If you two are going to
quarrel, I'm off to bed.

[*Exit* MRS THORVALD, *L.*]

ERIC. I'm sorry, Aunt Martha. I didn't mean to hurt your
feelings.

MARTHA. Don't apologize to me. Apologize to the Leader. It's
him you hurt when you talk like that. He cares so much
for all of us. . . . Goodnight, my Leader! God keep
you!

135

[*She salutes the picture and exit, L.*]

ERIC [*rises from his chair, goes up to the picture and regards it*]. Tell me, what is it you really want? Why do you make that fierce face? You're not fierce, really. You have eyes like my father's. Are you lonely, are you unhappy, behind that alarming beard? Yes, I see you are. Perhaps you only want love—like me. . . .

[*He continues to examine the picture.*]

COL. HUSSEK [*waking up with a violent start*]. Extend on the right! Rapid fire! Charge! [*Rubbing his eyes.*] Louisa! [*Enter* MRS VRODNY, *R.*] Where's my supper?

MRS VRODNY. We're waiting for Oswald.

COL. HUSSEK. Boozing again, I suppose!

MRS VRODNY. It's always the same thing, when he gets his pension-money.

[OSWALD'S *voice is heard singing, outside.*]

Here he is, at last!

[*Enter* OSWALD VRODNY, *drunk, R.*]

OSWALD [*singing*]. Then up spoke Captain O'Hara:
    'It's a hundred and one in the shade;
    If you give me your Irish whisky
    You can keep your Irish maid!'
Well, Louisa, and how are the busy little fingers, this evening? Good evening, General Fieldboots! Still fighting to the last man?

COL. HUSSEK. You're drunk, Sir!

OSWALD [*producing a bottle*]. I've brought you some powerful reinforcements! Guess what this is!

MRS VRODNY [*trying to snatch bottle*]. Give me that at once!

OSWALD. Naughty! Mustn't snatch! Allow me to introduce you to an old friend you haven't seen for a very long time— the finest Westland whisky!

COL. HUSSEK. How dare you bring their filthy stuff into this house!

MRS VRODNY. It's so unpatriotic!

OSWALD. Patriotism be damned! I can't touch that foul Ostnian cognac; sooner drink cold tea! What good is it going to do Ostnia if I ruin my liver? Answer me that! You and your patriotism! Those chaps over there know how to make whisky, and I'm grateful to them! Any man who makes good whisky is my friend for life! [*Drinks.*] Here's to Westland!

COL. HUSSEK. Another word, Sir, and I'll call the police and have you arrested, this minute!

MRS VRODNY. Father and I have been very patient with you. But there's a limit to everything. You've never done a hand's turn in your life! You're just a drunken sponger!

[*Enter* ANNA, *R.* ERIC *immediately turns from the picture, and begins to watch her, as before, but with increasing agitation.*]

ANNA. Mother! Mother! Do be quiet, please. All the neighbours will hear you! Come on, Uncle Oswald. Supper's ready in the kitchen.

OSWALD [*taking* ANNA'S *arm*]. That's my own little girl!

ANNA. You two go on. I'll look after him.

[*Exeunt* MRS VRODNY, *wheeling* COL. HUSSEK, *R.* ANNA *follows, half-supporting* OSWALD, *who is humming the Wedding March from Lohengrin.*]

ERIC [*taking a pace forward exclaims involuntarily, despairingly*]. Anna!

[*But* ANNA *does not seem to hear him. Exeunt* ANNA *and* OSWALD, *R.* ERIC *stands looking sadly after her.*]

CURTAIN

ACT II

ACT II

SCENE I

[*The Ostnia-Westland Room. It is evening. As the curtain rises, we see on the L. of the stage,* DR THORVALD, MRS THORVALD, MARTHA *and* ERIC, *drinking a bedtime cup of tea.* ERIC, *as usual, is watching* ANNA VRODNY, *who sits sewing on the R. of the stage, with* OSWALD *and* COL. HUSSEK. COL. HUSSEK *has the newspaper.* OSWALD *is lazily smoking. Both wireless-sets are switched on, but silent.*]

ANNA. Please come to bed, Grandpa. It's after eleven. You look tired out.

COL. HUSSEK. Nonsense, my dear! Never felt better in my life! Must wait to hear the news. Westland will have to admit responsibility. She can't get round the evidence. I tell you, this means war!

OSWALD. Thank God I'm fat and fifty! No more wars for us, Colonel! We've done our share!

COL. HUSSEK. I never thought I'd hear a nephew of mine confess to being a coward! It's the greatest regret of my life that I——

ANNA. Oh, Grandfather, don't excite yourself! You know he doesn't mean it. . . . Uncle Oswald, you mustn't be such a tease!

OSWALD. Well, you don't want Grandpa to be killed, do you? Or even your lazy old Uncle, I hope? Throw me the matches, there's a good girl.

[ANNA *does so.*]

MRS THORVALD. I think I *will* have a second cup, Martha, after all. I shan't sleep a wink, in any case. . . . Eric, dear, you haven't touched yours. Don't you want it?

ERIC. No, thank you, Mother.

Mrs Thorvald. Well, it *has* been a day of excitements! Those poor, poor children! I shall never dare to go by bus again! I suppose Ostnia will apologize. . . .

Dr Thorvald. They'll have to! The evidence of their guilt is overwhelming.

Martha. You can't apologize for murder! They must be punished!

[*Both wireless-sets give the time signal.*]

Dr Thorvald. Ssh! The news is coming on!

Anna [*calling*]. Mother! The news!

Westland Radio. Maria Kinderheim, the six-year-old child injured in the bomb outrage at the Iron Bridge, died in hospital this evening. This brings the number of the Westland dead up to nineteen.

[*Enter* Mrs Vrodny, *R.*]

Ostnian Radio. Peter Vollard, the eighty-year-old labourer injured in the bomb outrage at the Iron Bridge, died in hospital this evening. This brings the number of the Ostnian dead up to twenty.'

Westland Radio. The Minister for Propaganda and the Minister for Air and Marine flew to Castle Tuborg this afternoon to discuss with the Leader what steps should be taken. . . . It is rumoured that the Ostnian Government is calling up the nineteen-fourteen and nineteen-fifteen classes.

Ostnian Radio. An emergency meeting of the Cabinet was called this evening to consider what steps should be taken. . . . There are rumours that Westland will order general mobilization.

Westland Radio. In view of the extreme gravity of the situation . . .

Ostnian Radio. In view of the extreme gravity of the situation . . .

Westland Radio. The Leader . . .

Ostnian Radio. His Majesty the King . . .

Westland Radio. Has decided . . .

OSTNIAN RADIO. Has graciously consented . . .
WESTLAND RADIO. To address the nation . . .
OSTNIAN RADIO. To address his people . . .
WESTLAND RADIO. The address will be broadcast from all
stations at midnight.
OSTNIAN RADIO. The address will be broadcast from all stations
at midnight.

> [*Throughout the scene which follows, the two wireless
> sets provide a background of faint, disturbing ominous
> music.*]

MRS VRODNY. When I think of that poor old man who never
did anybody any harm, it makes my blood boil!

> [MARTHA *starts collecting the tea things.*]

MRS THORVALD. The poor mite! She was only a tiny tot!
ANNA. It's horrible! How can anyone have been such a brute!
MRS VRODNY. All Westlanders are brutes, dear.
ANNA. Some of them were killed, too; weren't they, Mother?
MRS VRODNY. How do you know? The papers don't say so.
The Westlanders are such liars, anyhow!
MRS THORVALD. The demonstration in the market square was
enormous. I could hardly push my way through!
DR THORVALD. I've never seen the students so moved. We had
to suspend all lectures for the day.
MRS VRODNY. There was a crowd outside Benets' this after-
noon. They were smashing the windows.
COL. HUSSEK. Serve them right! We don't want any dirty
Westlanders here, cheating us out of our money! Most of
them are spies! It's high time we cleared out the lot!
OSWALD. Well, I never did care for Westland much. The women
have thick ankles. All the same, I hope they don't sack
Freddy from the Long Bar. He mixes the best cocktails in
Ostnia.

> [*Exit* MARTHA, *L., with tray.*]

MRS THORVALD. I met Bob Veigel in the street, today. Such a

143

nice boy! And quite high up in his shock-troop already. He was so upset. I could hardly get a word out of him except: 'We must avenge the Iron Bridge!'

COL. HUSSEK. We must have action! You can't bandy words with murderers! We must avenge the Iron Bridge!

ANNA. I think I'll be going to bed, Mother. I've got rather a headache.

[*Re-enter* MARTHA, *L.*]

MRS VRODNY. But aren't you going to stay and hear the King?

ANNA. I don't think I will, Mother, if you don't mind. Goodnight. Goodnight, Uncle. Goodnight, Grandpa.

[*She hurries out, R., as if anxious to escape from them all.*]

MRS VRODNY. She's been so quiet all day. I'm afraid she's not well.

MRS THORVALD. Eric, dear, you're very silent, this evening. Aren't you feeling well?

ERIC [*abruptly*]. I've got a headache. I'm going to bed.

MARTHA. But Eric, the Leader!

MRS THORVALD. Oh, Martha! Don't worry him tonight! You can tell him all about it in the morning. [*To* ERIC.] You'll find some aspirin in the top drawer of my dressing-table.

ERIC. Thanks, Mother. Goodnight.

[*Exit, L.*]

MRS THORVALD. It must have been a very tiring day for him, with all these demonstrations.

DR THORVALD. I wonder. . . . I'm not very happy about him, Hilda. I'm afraid he's making some unhealthy friendships. They play at being radicals, pacifists, goodness knows what. Eric's such a child. He doesn't realize what this business means. This crime strikes at the whole basis of European civilization.

144

MRS VRODNY. Did you read Father Ambrose's article on the consequences of heresy? We must defend the Church. The Church is in danger!

OSWALD. I was taken to a service in Westland, once. God, I was bored! All those extempore prayers!

MARTHA. The Ostnians *aren't* civilized. They're savages! They burn incense and worship idols!

[*Noise and singing and the tramp of marching feet L. and R., off. All the characters move excitedly towards their respective windows, COL. HUSSEK propelling himself in his invalid chair. From this moment the acting works up to a note of hysteria.*]

MRS VRODNY [*at window, R.*]. Look, Father! The Air Force cadets!

MRS THORVALD [*at window, L.*]. It's the students! Hundreds of them!

OSWALD. They're tight!

MARTHA. The hour is at hand!

COL. HUSSEK. Stout fellows!

MRS THORVALD. How happy they look in their uniforms! I wish Eric was among them!

[*The two songs which follow should be sung simultaneously*].

WESTLAND STUDENTS [*off, L.*].

Brightly the sun on our weapons is gleaming,
     Brave is the heart and stout is the arm,
Gone is the night of talking and dreaming,
     Up and defend your country from harm!

The mountain has strength, the river has beauty,
     Westland Science, Religion and Art
Inspire us with valour and Westland Duty
     Echoes in every Westland heart!

Foremost of all the Leader is riding,
    Love in his bosom and truth on his brow,
Against the whole world in the Leader confiding,
    Forward to victory follow him now!

OSTNIAN AIR CADETS [*off, R.*].

Wheel the plane out from its shed,
Though it prove my funeral bed!
I'm so young. No matter, I
Will save my country ere I die!

Hark, I hear the engines roar!
Kiss me, we shall meet no more.
I must fly to north and south.
Kiss me, sweetheart, on the mouth!

Far from Mother, far from crowds,
I must fight among the clouds
Where the searchlights mow the sky,
I must fight and I must die!

DR THORVALD. It's the spirit of Pericles! The poets have not
    sung in vain!
MRS VRODNY. I wish I were a man!
MARTHA. Out of the pit! Out of the mire and clay!
OSWALD. Perhaps I ought to do something!
MRS THORVALD. The cards did not lie!
COL. HUSSEK. This makes me feel a boy again!
DR THORVALD. Some people have asked the meaning of history.
    They have their answer!
MRS VRODNY. They looked like princes!
MARTHA. The righteous shall inherit the earth!
OSWALD. I shall drink less and less!
MRS THORVALD. My headache's quite gone!
MRS VRODNY. We shall be very famous indeed!
MRS THORVALD. We shall never die!
COL. HUSSEK. I have never lost a battle!
DR THORVALD. Everything's perfectly clear, now!

146

OSWALD. After this, we shall all be much richer!

COL. HUSSEK. We are doing splendidly!

MARTHA. God is very glad!

OSTNIAN RADIO. This is Ostnia calling the world!

WESTLAND RADIO. This is Westland calling the world!

OSTNIAN RADIO. His Majesty the King!

WESTLAND RADIO. The Leader!

KING'S VOICE [*through radio, R.*]. It is hard to find words to express . . .

LEADER'S VOICE [*through radio, L.*]. The unceasing struggle of my life has been rewarded . . .

KING. How deeply touched we have been . . .

LEADER. Westland is restored to her greatness . . .

KING. By all the offers of service and sacrifice . . .

LEADER. One heart, one voice, one nation . . .

KING. Which have poured in from every corner of Our country . . .

LEADER. It is a lie to say that Westland has ever stooped to baseness . . .

KING. And from every class of people, even the poorest . . .

LEADER. It is a lie to say that Westland *could* ever stoop to baseness . . .

KING. These last few days of terrible anxiety have brought us all very close together . . .

LEADER. It is a lie to say that Westland wants war . . .

KING. We all, I know, pray from the bottom of our hearts . . .

LEADER. Westland stands in Europe as a great bastion . . .

KING. That this crisis may pass away . . .

LEADER. Against the tide of anarchy . . .

KING. Our Ministers are doing everything in their power . . .

LEADER. Westland lives and Westland soil are sacred . . .

KING. To avoid any irreparable step . . .

LEADER. Should any human power dare to touch either . . .

KING. But should the worst happen . . .

LEADER. It will have to face the holy anger of a nation in arms . . .

KING. We shall face it in a spirit worthy of the great traditions of our fathers . . .

LEADER. That will not sheathe the sword . . .

KING. To whom honour was more precious than life itself . . .

LEADER. Till it has paid for its folly with its blood . . .

KING. We stand before the bar of history . . .

LEADER. For, were Westland to suffer one unrequited wrong . . .

KING. Confident that right must triumph . . .

LEADER. I should have no wish to live!

KING. And we shall endure to the end!

> [*The wireless-sets play their respective national anthems.*]

COL. HUSSEK [*standing up in his chair, in great excitement*]. God save the King! God save the King!

> [*He collapses.*]

MRS VRODNY. Father! [*She runs to him.*] Quick, Oswald, the brandy!

MRS THORVALD. Dear me, I feel quite exhausted!

OSWALD [*looking in cupboard*]. There's no brandy left. He'll have to have my whisky.

MRS VRODNY. Hurry!

> [OSWALD *gives her the bottle and a glass.*]

Here, Father! [*Gives* HUSSEK *a sip.*] Take this.

DR THORVALD. Time we all went to bed. There won't be any more news tonight. Come along, Hilda.

COL. HUSSEK [*faintly, opening his eyes*]. Thank you, my dear . . . Sorry . . . My heart, again . . . Better now . . . It's been a great day . . .

MRS VRODNY [*to* OSWALD]. Help me to get him to bed.

MRS THORVALD. You're not staying up, are you, Martha dear?

MARTHA. I'll follow you in a minute.

OSWALD [*pushing the* COLONEL'S *chair*]. Up we go!

> [*Exeunt* DR *and* MRS THORVALD, *L.*]

Feeling better now? That whisky's wonderful stuff!

> [*Exeunt* OSWALD *and* COLONEL, *R., followed by* MRS

148

VRODNY *who turns out the light, so that the R. of the stage is darkened.*]

MARTHA [*kneeling before the* LEADER'S *portrait*]. My hero! My Leader! You will fight them, won't you? Say you will! Say you will! [*Kneels for a moment, then rises, salutes and exit L., turning out light.*]

[*The whole stage is now in complete darkness for some moments. Distant, dreamy music, off. Then a spotlight illuminates a small area in the middle of the stage. The various chairs and tables should have been pushed back, so that they are visible only as indistinct shapes in the surrounding darkness. Enter* ERIC *and* ANNA, *L. and R. respectively. They advance slowly, like sleep-walkers, until they stand just outside the circle of light, facing each other.*]

ERIC. Is that you, Anna?
ANNA. Yes, Eric.

[*They both take a step forward into the light-circle.*]

ERIC. I knew I could make this happen!
ANNA. Where are we?
ERIC. In the place that I have found for us,
    The place that I have hoped for since I was born,
    Born, as we all are, into a world full of fear,
    Where the faces are not the faces of the happy,
    Where the disappointed hate the young
    And the disinherited weep in vain.
    Not that any are wanting this world, any;
    The truckdriver, the executive setting his watch,
    The clerk entraining for the office, us,
    All of us wishing always it were different.
    All of us wanting to be kind and honest,
    Good neighbours and good parents and good children,
    To be beautiful and likeable and happy.
    Ever since I was born I have been looking,
    Looking for a place where I could really be myself,

149

For a person who would see me as I really am.

And I have found them both, found them now, found them here.

This is the good place.

ANNA. I am afraid. The darkness is so near.

ERIC. This is the good place

Where the air is not filled with screams of hatred

Nor words of great and good men twisted

To flatter conceit and justify murder.

Here are no family quarrels or public meetings,

No disease or old age. No death.

Here we can be really alone,

Alone with our love, our faith, our knowledge,

I've struggled for this ever since I saw you.

A long time, Anna. Did you know that?

ANNA. A long time, Eric, yes, I've felt you near me.

You took my arm in crowded shops,

Helping me choose.

Behind my chair as I sat sewing, you stood

And gave me patience. Often you sat

Beside me in the park and told me stories

Of couples in the panting unfair city

Who loved each other all their lives.

O when I went to dances, all my partners

Were you, were you.

ERIC. Ever since I remember I've caught glimpses of you,

At first, far off, a nature on the crag,

Far off down the long poplar avenue, a traveller.

I've seen your face reflected in the river

As I sat fishing; and when I read a book

Your face would come between me and the print

Like an ambition, nearer and clearer every day.

And now, at last . . .

ANNA. Do They see, too?

ERIC. They do not want to see. Their blindness is

Their pride, their constitution and their town

Where Love and Truth are movements underground

Dreading arrest and torture.

150

ANNA. O Eric, I'm so afraid of them!

ERIC. Locked in each other's arms, we form a tower
    They cannot shake or enter. Our love
    Is the far and unsuspected island
    Their prestige does not hold.

ANNA. I wish that this could last for ever.

ERIC. It can, Anna, it can! Nothing matters now
    But you and I. This is the everlasting garden
    Where we shall walk together always,
    Happy, happy, happy, happy.

ANNA. You do not know their power. They know, know all.
    They let us meet but only to torment us
    When they have proved our guilt. They grin behind our
        joy,
    Waiting their time. O if we take one step
    Towards our love, the grace will vanish,
    Our peace smash like a vase. O we shall see
    The threatening faces sudden at the window, hear
    The furious knocking on the door,
    The cry of anger from the high-backed chair.

ERIC. It can't be true! It shan't be true!
    Our love is stronger than their hate!
    Kiss me.

ANNA. Don't, don't! You'll make them angry!
    We shall be punished!

ERIC. I don't care! I defy them!

[*He steps forward to embrace her. The stage is immediately plunged in darkness. Their voices now begin to
grow fainter.*]

VOICES [*These should be taken by the actors playing* DR THOR-
VALD *and* MRS VRODNY, *and should have the resonant
disembodied quality of an echo*]. NO!

ERIC'S VOICE: Anna, Anna. Where are you?

ANNA'S VOICE. Where are you, Eric?

ERIC. Come back.

ANNA. I can't. They're too strong. Help me, Eric. They're
taking me away.

VOICE 1. Take her away.

ERIC. They're holding me back.

VOICE 2. Hold him back.

ANNA. I shall never see you again.

BOTH VOICES. Never see } him her { again.

ERIC. Anna. Can you hear me? I swear I'll come back to you. I'll beat them somehow. Only wait for me, Anna. Promise you'll wait.

ANNA. I promise, Eric.

VOICE 2 [*whispering*]. Tradition and breeding count.

VOICE 1 [*whispering*]. You can't wipe out the history of a thousand years.

CURTAIN

(BEFORE THE CURTAIN)

[Five men, three women. Three couples are waltzing. The two remaining men, who are supposed to be left-wing political workers, are watching, in the background.]

FIRST MALE DANCER.

The papers say there'll be war before long;
Sometimes they're right, and sometimes they're wrong.

SECOND MALE DANCER.

There's a lot of talk in a wireless-set
And a lot more promised than you'll ever get.

FIRST LEFTIST.

Don't believe them,
Only fools let words deceive them.
Resist the snare, the scare
Of something that's not really there.
These voices commit treason
Against all truth and reason,
Using an unreal aggression
To blind you to your real oppression;
Truth is elsewhere.
Understand the motive, penetrate the lie
Or you will die.

THIRD MALE DANCER.

The Winter comes, the Summer goes;
If there's a war, we shall fight, I suppose.

FIRST MALE DANCER.

The larder is cold, the kitchen is hot;
If we go we'll be killed, if we don't we'll be shot.

SECOND LEFTIST.

What they can do depends on you,
You are many, they are few,
Afraid for their trade, afraid
Of the overworked and the underpaid.
Do not go; they know

153

That though they seem so strong
Their power lasts so long
As you are undecided and divided;
Understand the wrong;
Understand the fact;
Unite and act.

SECOND MALE DANCER.

There're hills in the north and sea in the south;
It's wiser not to open your mouth.

THIRD MALE DANCER.

Soldiers have guns and are used in attack;
More of them go than ever come back.

FIRST FEMALE DANCER.

What shall I say to the child at my knee
When you fall in the mountains or sink in the sea?

SECOND FEMALE DANCER.

What shall we do if you lose a leg?
Sing for our supper, or steal or beg?

FIRST LEFTIST.

It's weak to submit,
Then cry when you are hit.
It's mad to die
For what you know to be a lie.
And whom you kill
Depends upon your will.
Their blood is upon your head.
Choose to live.
The dead cannot forgive
Nor will time pardon the dead.

THIRD FEMALE DANCER.

What is a parlour, what is a bed
But a place to weep in when you are dead?

FIRST MALE DANCER.

It's goodbye to the bench and goodbye to the wife
And goodbye for good to somebody's life.

SECOND MALE DANCER.

Our country's in danger, and our cause is just;
If no one's mistaken, it's conquer or bust.

154

SECOND LEFTIST.
    The country is in danger
    But not from any stranger.
    Your enemies are here
    Whom you should fight, not fear
    For till they cease
    The earth will know no peace.
    Learn to know
    Your friend from your foe.
THIRD MALE DANCER.
    But if someone's mistaken or lying or mad,
    Or if we're defeated, it will be just too bad.

BLACK OUT

155

ACT II

SCENE II

[VALERIAN'S *study. Just after midnight.*]

> [VALERIAN *and* STAHL, *with brandy glasses before them, are listening to the* LEADER'S *speech on the radiogram.*]

LEADER'S VOICE. . . . . it will have to face the holy anger of a nation in arms, that will not sheathe the sword till it has paid for its folly with its blood. For, were Westland to suffer one unrequited wrong, I should have no wish to live!

VALERIAN. Admirable sentiments! A little more brandy, my dear Stahl?

STAHL. Thanks. . . . I need it. . . . [*Pours and drinks.*] The man's got a voice like a corncrake!

VALERIAN. Oh, I can't agree with you there! His delivery is really excellent. He has mastered all the tricks. I'm told that he once took lessons from Sacha Guitry.

STAHL. I didn't like the tone of that speech at all. . . . You know he saw the General Staff again, this evening? You mark my words, this is to prepare the country for mobilization. The decree's probably signed already.

VALERIAN. Hammel would never agree to it.

STAHL. Then he'll override Hammel. We're dealing with a madman. You said so, yourself.

VALERIAN. Very well. Let us suppose that mobilization is ordered. What does that mean, nowadays? Nothing! We live in an age of bluff. The boys shout until they are hoarse, and the politicians hunt for a formula under the conference-table. A lot of noise to cover up an enormous cold funk.

STAHL. Cold funk is an exceedingly dangerous state of mind. A coward often hits first.

VALERIAN. But, I ask you, who wants war? Certainly not the industrialists: the arms race is good for another five years at least. Certainly not the politicians: they're far too jealous of the military and afraid of losing their jobs. Even the General Staffs don't want it: they're both perfectly happy playing at mechanization. . . . Do you seriously imagine that wars nowadays are caused by some escaped lunatic putting a bomb under a bridge and blowing up an omnibus? There have been worse provocations in the past, and there will be worse in the future. The national honour will swallow them all quite conveniently. It has a very strong digestion.

[*Enter* LESSEP, *R., with papers.*]

LESSEP. Here are the latest press bulletins, Mr Valerian.
VALERIAN. Thank you.

[*Reads. Exit* LESSEP. *R.*]

STAHL. Anything fresh?
VALERIAN. Nothing. Students' demonstrations. Patriotic speeches. All the customary nonsense. . . . Our operatives gathered outside the Villa Kismet during the lunch hour and cheered the Leader till it was time to go back to work. Then two of the organizers of the illegal trades union were recognized in the crowd, and so roughly handled that the Police had to take them into preventive custody. . . . The Iron Bridge incident has certainly solved some of our labour problems—for the moment.
STAHL. Yes—for the moment. . . . But, even supposing that there's no war, how will all this end?
VALERIAN. It will end itself. In ten days there will be a new distraction—an international football match or a girl found murdered in her bath. . . . [*Reads.*] This is rather amusing. An Ostnian journalist has written an article proving conclusively that the Iron Bridge bomb was fired by order of myself!
STAHL. Haha! Thank goodness for something to laugh at, anyway!
VALERIAN. 'The sinister Westland industrialists, realizing that

157

they have brought their country to the verge of ruin, attempt a desperate gambler's throw' . . . You know, Stahl, a crime of this sort—so pointless, so entirely without motive—is bound to have a curious psychological effect upon everybody. Don't *you* sometimes wake up in the night, and wonder: Who did it? Like the reader of a detective story? And, of course, the most apparently innocent are the most suspect. Perhaps it was the Ostnian archbishop. Perhaps it was the wife of our municipal librarian. Perhaps it was my butler, Manners. And then, inevitably, one begins to wonder: was it I myself, in a moment of insanity, followed by amnesia? Have I an alibi? Ought I to go to the Police and confess? Madness is so infectious.

STAHL. In your list of suspects, you've forgotten the chief madman. Why shouldn't it have been the Leader, himself?

VALERIAN. Ah, no, my friend. The Leader is the only man in all Westland who is quite above suspicion. If he had done it, he would never have been able to resist telling us so! [*Listening.*] I wonder who that is on the stairs? Surely it can't be a visitor, at this hour of the night?

[*Enter* MANNERS, *R.*]

MANNERS. It's the Leader, Sir.

STAHL. Gracious! I'd better clear out.

VALERIAN. No. Please stay. This will be interesting.

[*Enter the* LEADER *and Storm-Trooper* GRIMM, *R. The* LEADER's *whole manner has changed. He is obviously exhausted. He speaks gently, almost timidly. Storm-Trooper* GRIMM *takes up his position at the back of the stage. Throughout the scene which follows, he neither moves nor speaks.*]

LEADER. May I come in?

VALERIAN. This is an unexpected honour.

LEADER. I saw your light in the window, on my way back from the Broadcasting Station.

VALERIAN. We have been listening to your speech.

LEADER [*sinking into a chair*]. How quiet it is, in here! All day

long I have been surrounded by shouting, noise, crowds.
I thought: for a few moments I shall be able to be quiet. . . .

STAHL. Perhaps, my Leader, you'd prefer to be left alone?

LEADER. No, no. I hate to be alone. Don't leave me, any of
you. . . .

VALERIAN. You must be very tired?

LEADER. More tired than I have ever been, in my whole life.

VALERIAN. You'll take some wine? Something to eat?

> [*The* LEADER *does not reply.* VALERIAN *makes a sign
> to* MANNERS, *who goes out, R.*]

LEADER [*begins to speak quietly, then with rising hysteria*]. For
five nights I have lain awake, wondering: What shall I do?
What shall I do? And no one can decide for me. No one!
I alone must make the final choice. Peace or war? It is a
terrible burden to put upon the shoulders of one man. . . .
You think I am strong? No, I am weak, weak. . . . I never
wished to be the Leader. It was forced upon me. Forced
upon me, I tell you, by the men who said they were my
friends, and who thought only of their own ambition.
They made use of me. They made use of my love for my
dear country. They never loved Westland as I did. . . . I
stood on a platform in a village hall or a table in a little
restaurant—when I began to speak, people listened. More
and more people. It was like a dream. I was proud of my
power. They flattered me. . . . And I was so simple; only
a poor out-of-work bank-clerk. I believed them. . . . My
parents were country people. They gave their last savings
to have me educated. 'You mustn't grow up to be a
peasant,' they told me. And I obeyed them. I worked hard.
I would have been contented with so little. I was afraid
of the world, of the rich people in their fine houses. I
feared them and I hated them. . . . And then I found that
I could speak. It was easy. So easy. I had money, friends.
They told me: 'You will be a great man.' I learnt their
ways. Step by step. Climbing higher and higher. I had to
be cunning. I had to do horrible things. I had to intrigue
and murder. Nobody knows that I did it all for Westland.
Only for Westland. . . . Don't you believe me?

VALERIAN [*soothingly*]. Certainly we believe you.

LEADER. In the nights, when my people are all asleep, I lie and tremble. You would never understand. . . . It's like some terrible nightmare. I—I alone, am responsible. And at the great receptions, when I stand there in my uniform, with all the foreign diplomats and the beautiful well-born women around me (the women I used to dream of when I was a poor boy in an office), I want to scream in all their faces: 'Leave me alone! Leave me alone! Let me go back to my parents' cottage! Let me be humble and free!' Some of these women know what I am feeling. I see it in their eyes. How they despise me! [*Screaming.*] Don't you see how you are all torturing me? I can't bear it! I must bear it! I can't bear it! [*Covers his face with his hands and sobs.*] No! No! No! No!

> [VALERIAN *goes quietly over to the radiogram, and starts the record of Rameau's Tambourin. Then he and* STAHL *remain motionless, watching the* LEADER. *During the music,* MANNERS *comes in, R., silently places a tray of cold supper near the* LEADER'S *chair, and exit, R.*]

> [*As the music proceeds, the* LEADER'S *sobbing quietens and stops. For some time he remains motionless, his face in his hands. Then, slowly, he raises his head. His expression is now calm and radiant. When the music stops, he is smiling.*]

LEADER. Ah . . . that music! How clearly I see the way now! [*Rising to his feet.*] Listen, all of you. I have made a great decision! Tomorrow morning, the whole world will hear that I have withdrawn the Westland troops, unconditionally, ten miles from the frontier. It will hear that I have proposed to Ostnia a pact of non-aggression, guaranteeing the sanctity of the frontier for a thousand years!

STAHL. My Leader, may I congratulate you? This is the finest thing you have ever done!

LEADER. They will not sneer at me any more, will they, in England and France and America? They will not be able to say I wanted war. My decision will be famous. It will be praised in the history books. I will make my country the greatest of all gifts—the gift of peace!

STAHL. This is magnificent!

LEADER. Tomorrow night, you will hear my greatest speech. My Peace Speech. I shall stand before my shock troopers and I shall tell them: War is glorious, but Peace is more glorious still! And I shall convince them! I know it! I am strong, now! They may not understand at first, but they will obey, because it is my will. The will of their Leader. The immutable, unconquerable will of the Westland nation. . . . I must speak to General Staff Headquarters, at once!

STAHL [*aside*]. Valerian, you have saved us all!

VALERIAN [*aside*]. I receive your thanks on behalf of poor Rameau. If only he were alive! How very surprised he would be!

[*Enter* LESSEP, *R., with envelope.*]

LESSEP. My Leader, an urgent despatch from General Staff Headquarters.

LEADER [*reads, crumples paper. Furiously*]. They have dared! You will bear witness, all of you, that Westland had no hand in this! You will record my decision for the judgment of posterity!

STAHL. But—my Leader, what has happened?

LEADER. An hour ago, the Ostnian troops crossed our frontier! Kapra has been bombed by Ostnian planes. Women and children foully, heartlessly murdered!

STAHL. Oh, my God!

VALERIAN. The idiots!

LEADER. The die is cast! The name of Ostnia shall be blotted from the map of Europe for ever!

STAHL. This is the end of everything!

LEADER [*in his platform manner*]. Confident in the justice of our cause, and determined to defend our sacred Westland homesteads to the last, we swear——

[*He is still shouting as the* CURTAIN *falls.*]

161

ACT III

ACT III

SCENE I

[*The Ostnia-Westland Room. It is early evening. On the L. of stage, MARTHA sits rolling bandages. MRS THORVALD is knitting a muffler. DR THORVALD is reading the casualty-lists in the newspaper.*]

> [*On the R. of the stage sits MRS VRODNY, all in black, alone. She is staring in front of her, with a fixed expression. She looks much older.*]
>
> [*It is noticeable that both homes seem shabbier and poorer than in the earlier scenes. Several pieces of furniture are missing. Indeed, the VRODNY-HUSSEK home is almost bare.*]

MRS THORVALD. Mrs Veigal says it was perfectly wonderful. She could hear Bob's voice just as if he were in the room. He told her not to worry. Those who have passed over are all very happy. He said the Other Side was difficult to describe, but it was like listening to glorious music!

MARTHA. It's wicked, Hilda; and dangerous as well! How does she know she wasn't talking to an evil spirit?

MRS THORVALD. I don't see that it can do any harm. And it's such a comfort to her! Poor woman, she idolized Bob!

DR THORVALD. Well, at least she can be proud of him! Listen to this: 'Robert Veigal. Killed in action. December the tenth. The Blue Order. For conspicuous gallantry in the face of the enemy.' The casualty-lists this evening are terrible! That offensive on the Slype Canal was a shambles. If they don't make some big changes on the General Staff soon, there'll be trouble! Hammel ought to have been retired years ago.

MARTHA. There're too many healthy young men slacking in cushy staff jobs! As for those cowardly pacifists, I can't think why they're allowed to have a soft time in prison! They ought to be sent to the firing-line!

Mrs Thorvald. Oh, Martha, you're cruel! After all, Eric's your nephew!

Dr Thorvald. Hilda, I've told you before never to mention his name in this house again! The shame of it has almost killed me!

Mrs Thorvald. I suppose you wish he'd been blown to pieces by a shell, like Bob Veigal! Well, perhaps he *is* dead! They wouldn't tell me anything!

Dr Thorvald. You didn't go to the prison?

Mrs Thorvald. Yes I did! So there! He's my son and I want to see him! I don't care about anything, any more. . . . Eric, my darling boy, what have they done to you?

[*She bursts into tears.*]

Dr Thorvald. She's overwrought. She doesn't know what she's saying. . . . Martha, could you make some coffee? It would do her good.

Martha. We haven't any coffee. And we've used up our week's ration of sugar, already. There isn't any more firewood, either.

Dr Thorvald. I suppose we shall have to burn another of the spare-room chairs. [*With an attempt to smile.*] Soon we shall be sitting on the floor!

Martha. I'll see what I can find.

[*Exit, L.*]

Dr Thorvald [*rising and going over to his wife*]. I'm sorry, dear!

Mrs Thorvald [*sobbing*]. You're not! You don't love Eric! You never did!

Dr Thorvald. Perhaps I have been rather harsh. I haven't tried to understand what made him act as he did. You see, I was brought up to think that a man's greatest privilege was to fight for his country; and it's hard to change one's ideas. Perhaps we were all wrong. War seems so beastly when it actually happens! Perhaps 'country' and 'frontier'

166

are old-fashioned words that don't mean anything now. What are we really fighting for? I feel so muddled! It's not so easy to rearrange one's beliefs, at our age. For we're both getting on, aren't we, dear? You must help me. We've got no one to turn to now, but each other. We must try to think of all the happy times we've had together. . . . You remember them too, don't you, Hilda? We must make a new start. . . . I tell you what I'll do—tomorrow I'll go down to the prison myself! Perhaps I shall be able to get something out of them!

MRS THORVALD [*looks up and smiles*]. Thank you, dear!

DR THORVALD. That's better! Give me a kiss! [*They embrace and remain seated together, holding hands.*] This is quite like old times, isn't it?

[*Enter* ANNA, *also in black, R.*]

MRS VRODNY [*without turning her head, in a harsh, croaking voice*]. How much did he give you?

ANNA. Eight hundred and fifty.

MRS VRODNY. That's ridiculous! It cost twelve hundred!

ANNA. Oh, Mother, I know! I argued and argued with him! But it was no use. He just laughed. I was so afraid he might refuse to take it at all. Then he tried to kiss me. . . . It was beastly!

MRS VRODNY. Your father gave me that brooch on our engagement day.

ANNA. Why did you do it, Mother? Wasn't there anything else?

MRS VRODNY. It was the last I had. But what does it matter?

ANNA. You're worn out. Why don't you take a day in bed? I'll look after everything.

MRS VRODNY. Nonsense! You've got your hospital-work to do. Aren't you on night-duty this week? You ought to be getting your things on, now.

ANNA. Very well, Mother.

[*Exit, R.*]

[*Enter* MARTHA, *with tray, L.*]

167

MARTHA. I've made you some herbal tea. It's all there is.

MRS THORVALD. How sweet of you, Martha! [*To* DR THORVALD.] I haven't had time to look at the paper yet. Is there any real news? They never tell us anything!

DR THORVALD. Nothing much. All the fronts were quiet, this morning. The usual rumours of desertion and mutinies in the Ostnian regiments. Probably nonsense. But there seems no doubt that they're having a very bad time with the Plague. They're dying by thousands, apparently!

MARTHA. It shows there's some justice in the world!

MRS THORVALD [*notices that there are only two cups on the tray*]. Won't you have a cup as well, Martha? You're not looking too grand, you know. Are you all right?

MARTHA. I've got a bad headache, that's all. I think perhaps a cup would do me good. I'm feeling so thirsty!

[*Exit, L.*]

DR THORVALD. Of course, the papers have censored it, but I hear that there've been one or two cases here, among the prisoners of war.

MRS THORVALD. Oliver! How dreadful! Supposing it spreads!

DR THORVALD. Oh, we're safe enough!

MRS THORVALD. But just suppose it does! What are the symptoms?

DR THORVALD. I don't know exactly. A swelling under the arm, I believe. . . . But you mustn't worry your head about that!

[*Enter* ANNA, *R., in nurse's uniform.*]

ANNA. I'm off now, Mother.

MRS VRODNY. Keep clear of the office when you go downstairs. They took away the caretaker, this morning.

ANNA [*hysterically*]. Can't they do anything to stop it, before it kills everybody in the whole world? It's taken Grandfather. It's taken Uncle Oswald. It'll take us, too, soon! What have we all done that we should be destroyed like this? Nobody's *alive* any more! I look at the faces in the streets, and they're not the faces of living people! We're all dead!

MRS VRODNY. Anna! Control yourself!

[*L. and R., as in Act II, Scene I, the sound of marching feet is heard. But this time there is no music, only the tap of a drum.*]

[ANNA *goes to window, R.*]

[*Enter* MARTHA, *L., with her cup.*]

MRS THORVALD. Those horrible drums! Oh, shut the window! I can't bear the sound any more!

DR THORVALD [*going to window, L.*]. They're mere boys! How many of them will be alive in a week's time? They used to sing once. . . . Oh, God, why can't it stop!

[*Bangs down window.*]

MRS VRODNY. Listen to them marching! Think what those men are going to face. Grandfather was a soldier, and his father before him. We're the only ones left now. Perhaps we shan't be here much longer. But remember that, whatever happens to you, you come of a family of soldiers! Never forget that!

[*The marching dies away.*]

DR THORVALD. I must be off to the University. We're working out a new scheme of courses for the blind. Can I get anything for you in town?

MARTHA. Could you get me some linament?

MRS THORVALD. Linament? What for, Martha? Have you hurt yourself?

MARTHA. I don't know. I've got such a funny swelling.

DR THORVALD [*exchanging a quick glance with his wife*]. A swelling?

MRS THORVALD. How long have you had it?

MARTHA. Only since this morning. It came up quite suddenly.

DR THORVALD. Could you have bruised yourself, somehow?

MARTHA. Oh no, I'm quite sure I haven't. . . . But it hurts!

DR THORVALD [*trying to speak calmly*]. Where, exactly, is this swelling, Martha?

MARTHA. Here. Under my arm. . . . Why, what's the matter?

MRS THORVALD [*jumping up with a scream*]. She's got it! She's

got the Plague! Don't let her touch me! Keep her away!
We shall catch it! We shall all die!

DR THORVALD. Quiet, Hilda! I don't expect it's anything
serious, but you'd better go to your room, Martha. . . .
I'll phone for the doctor at once!

[*He and his wife instinctively back away from*
MARTHA *into a corner of the stage.*]

MARTHA [*hysterical*]. No! No! It can't be! I won't! I've been
good! You can't let me die! I've never had a chance! You
don't know how I've suffered! You don't know what it's
like to be ugly, to see everyone else getting married, to
spend your life looking after other people's children! I've
sacrificed everything! I had brains! I might have had a
brilliant career, but I gave it all up for you! I've been
more loyal than any of them! If you let me die, there's no
point in being good, any more! It doesn't matter! It's all
a lie! I've never been happy! I've been betrayed!

ANNA [*as if listening to sounds in the very far distance*].
Mother . . . can't you hear them, over there? They're
crying, they're suffering—just like us!

MRS VRODNY [*speaking with a kind of terrible obstinacy,
which belies her words*]. I hear nothing!

MARTHA [*runs to the* LEADER'S *portrait*]. Oh, my Leader! Say
you don't mean it! Say I'm going to live! Speak to me!

[*She falls on her knees before the picture, and, in
doing so, switches on the wireless.*]

WESTLAND RADIO [*tonelessly, like a time-signal*]. Kill, Kill,
Kill, Kill, Kill! [*Continues to the end of scene.*]

ANNA [*with an involuntary despairing cry*]. Eric, where are you?

CURTAIN

(BEFORE THE CURTAIN)

[*Three Westland soldiers are grouped, L., behind some kind of simplified construction to represent a parapet. They stare across the stage into the darkness, R., where the Ostnian trenches are supposed to lie. The Ostnians remain invisible, throughout, but their voices are represented by the two remaining male members of the chorus, off. One of the Westland soldiers has an accordion, to which he sings:*]

FIRST SOLDIER.

> Ben was a four foot seven Wop,
> He worked all night in a bucket-shop
> On cocoa, and sandwiches,
> And bathed on Sunday evenings.
>
> In winter when the woods were bare
> He walked to work in his underwear
> With his hat in his hand,
> But his watch was broken.
>
> He met his Chief in the Underground,
> He bit him hard till he turned round
> In the neck, and the ear,
> And the left-hand bottom corner.
>
> He loved his wife though she was cruel,
> He gave her an imitation jewel
> In a box, a black eye,
> And a very small packet of Woodbines.

OSTNIAN [*off*]. The *only* brand!
SECOND SOLDIER. Ssh! Did you hear that?
FIRST SOLDIER. The bleeders! I'll show 'em. [*Picks up rifle.*]
THIRD SOLDIER. Sit down, yer fool. You'll start something.
    [*Shouts across stage.*] Hullo!

171

OSTNIAN [*off*]. Hullo!

THIRD SOLDIER. Wot's it like, your side?

OSTNIAN [*off*]. Wet.

THIRD SOLDIER. Same here.

OSTNIAN [*off*]. Got any cigarettes?

SECOND SOLDIER. Yes. But no ruddy matches.

OSTNIAN [*off*]. We've got matches, Swop?

SECOND SOLDIER. Right. Coming over. [*Throws matches.*]

OSTNIAN [*off*]. Thanks. Coming over. [*The packet of cigarettes
flies out of the darkness but falls short, outside the parapet.*]
Sorry!

FIRST SOLDIER. Christ, you Ostnians throw like a pack of
school-girls! [*To the others.*] Wait a mo. Gimme a torch.

SECOND SOLDIER. Take care!

FIRST SOLDIER. Oh, they're all right! [*Climbs over parapet and
looks for cigarettes.*]

OSTNIAN [*off*]. More to the left. Further. There, man! Right
under your nose!

FIRST SOLDIER. Got 'em. Thanks, boys. [*Picks up packet and
climbs back.*]

OSTNIAN [*singing, off*].

> What are we fighting for?
> What are we fighting for?

THIRD SOLDIER [*joining in*]. Only the sergeant knows. [*To* FIRST
SOLDIER.] Come on, Angel. Get yer squeeze-box.

[FIRST SOLDIER *begins to play the accordion. Air:
'Mademoiselle from Armentiers'. The three Westland
soldiers sing the first six verses in turn, all joining in
the chorus.*]

The biscuits are hard and the beef is high,
The weather is wet and the drinks are dry,
We sit in the mud and wonder why.

With faces washed until they shine
The G.H.Q. sit down to dine
A hundred miles behind the line.

The Colonel said he was having a doze;
I looked through the window; a rambler rose
Climbed up his knee in her underclothes.

The chaplain paid us a visit one day,
A shell came to call from over the way,
You should have heard the bastard pray!

The subaltern's heart was full of fire,
Now he hangs on the old barbed wire
All blown up like a motor-tyre.

The sergeant-major gave us hell.
A bullet struck him and he fell.
Where did it come from? Who can tell?

[*The* OSTNIANS *now join in.* OSTNIANS *and* WEST-
LANDERS *sing the following six verses alternately,
joining in the last.*]

Kurt went sick with a pain in his head,
Malingering, the Doctor said.
Gave him a pill. Next day he was dead.

Fritz was careless, I'm afraid.
He lost his heart to a parlour-maid.
Now he's lost his head to a hand-grenade.

Karl married a girl with big blue eyes.
He went back on leave; to his surprise
The hat in the hall was not his size.

Oh, No Man's Land is a pleasant place,
You can lie there as long as you lie on your face
Till your uniform is an utter disgrace.

I'd rather eat turkey than humble pie,
I'd rather see mother than lose an eye,
I'd rather kiss a girl than die.

We're sick of the rain and the lice and the smell,
We're sick of the noise of shot and shell,
And the whole bloody war can go to hell!

BLACK OUT

ACT III

SCENE II

[VALERIAN'S *study*. VALERIAN *is nervously pacing the room.* LESSEP *is seated by the desk, at the telephone. It is night.*]

VALERIAN. Call the hospital again. There must be some news by now!

LESSEP [*dials and speaks into phone*]. Hullo. . . . Is that the Central Hospital? Mr Valerian wishes to enquire for his butler, Mr Manners. . . . Thank you. . . .

VALERIAN. I told him not to go into the city; and he disobeyed me—for the first time! He risked his life, Lessep: and do you know why? To try and find me a pot of caviare! Ridiculous, isn't it? [*Going to window.*] Tell me, is the Plague really so bad, down there?

LESSEP. It's much worse than they admit. The newspapers are still ordered to minimize it; and they're burying all the dead by night.

VALERIAN. Extraordinary. . . . Up here, we inhabit another world!

LESSEP. But, Mr Valerian, there's always the danger of infection. Even for us! Forgive my speaking of it again, but don't you think it would be wiser to move? You could go to your villa at Konia. . . .

VALERIAN. If you are frightened you have my permission to go there—alone.

LESSEP. Of course, I'm only thinking of *your* safety. . . . [*Into telephone.*] Yes? Yes . . . Oh . . . I am very sorry. . . . Thank you. . . .

VALERIAN. Well, what do they say?

LESSEP. Manners . . . I'm afraid he's dead. . . . Half an hour ago. The fever didn't break.

VALERIAN. Dead. . . . So. . . . I'm sorry. . . . Well, there's nothing

175

I can do about it now. [*To* LESSEP.] Have any more reports
come in?

LESSEP. Only a telegram from the Tarnberg Colliery. The eight
o'clock shift refused to go down, and are threatening to
destroy the plant. The manager doesn't think the police
are reliable.

VALERIAN. Nothing from Headquarters?

LESSEP. There's been no news of any kind from the front all
day. The storm must have broken down the wires. [*Buzzer
on desk sounds.*]

VALERIAN. See who that is.

LESSEP [*into the house telephone*]. Hullo. Speaking. Yes, Mr
Valerian is here.

VALERIAN. Who is it?

LESSEP. It's Mr Stahl. He's coming upstairs now.

[*Enter* STAHL, *R. He is haggard and exhausted. His
clothes and raincoat are splashed with mud.*]

STAHL. Valerian! Thank God you're safe!

VALERIAN. My dear Stahl, this is a pleasant surprise. I thought
you were visiting our gallant boys in the trenches. Oh dear,
where *did* you get that cap? It makes you look like a racing
tout. And you're wet through. What have you been doing?
How did you get here?

STAHL. I managed to find the airfield. Thank God, most of the
pilots are still loyal. We landed in the meadows, a couple
of miles from the house. In the pitch darkness. . . . We
were lucky not to crash.

VALERIAN. What a state you're in! Lessep, the brandy.

STAHL. Thanks. . . . [*Drinks.*] I'm quite exhausted. Ran most of
the way through woods, over ploughed fields . . . didn't
dare show myself on the road. . . .

VALERIAN. I say, Stahl, are you tight? What *is* the matter?

STAHL. You mean, you don't know?

VALERIAN. There's been no news all day. The telegraph wires
are down.

STAHL. Cut, you mean. . . . When we were only a few miles from
the front the car was stopped by a couple of private

176

soldiers, we were told to get out, and taken along to a sort of barn. They wouldn't answer any questions, but there were a lot of officers in the barn, prisoners like myself, and I soon learnt what was happening. The whole Northern sector has mutinied and are fraternizing with the enemy. All officers who tried to stop them were shot out of hand. Jansen was bayoneted in his own headquarters. . . . And that's not all. There was a revolution in the Ostnian capital this morning. The King's hiding somewhere in the mountains; tomorrow he will have abdicated, if he's alive. The Ostnians have got loud-speakers in the front line, calling on their soldiers to make an armistice and revolt against their own government!

VALERIAN. Excellent! Nothing could be better. The new Ostnian government is certain to be incompetent and full of intrigue. It will be our big chance to finish things off. But I'm interrupting you. How did you get away?

STAHL. I managed to bribe one of the guards with a cigarette case.

VALERIAN. Not the one your wife gave you for a silver wedding present? My word, you'll catch it!

STAHL. Valerian, this isn't funny. This humour of yours is becoming a pose. We've got to get out of here. There's nothing either of us can do.

VALERIAN. And where do you propose that we should go?

STAHL. You know I had a cable the other day from Quinta in Rio, asking me to help him build up the South American Trusts? I'm going to accept his offer, and I want you to come too. We need you, Valerian.

VALERIAN. My dear friend, I am too old for carpet-bagging. Quinta would impose his own conditions. He'd use us like office boys.

STAHL. This is no time for false pride. Do you realize, man, that if you stay here you'll see your life-work ruined before your eyes?

VALERIAN. Steady, steady. Don't get hysterical. Listen, what you tell me doesn't surprise me in the least. I only wonder it hasn't happened before. What can you expect? The war should have been over in three weeks if our friend Hammel had the brains of a fifth-rate actor. It's gone on for nine months. The plague was bad luck certainly, but if our public health authorities had ever learnt to co-operate with each other, it could have been kept within bounds. Of course, there're mutinies and strikes; there'll be more before we're done. There were plenty in the Great War. . . . A lot of people will have to be arrested, and a few of them shot. The Leader will visit the trenches again in person. There'll be an advance of a hundred yards somewhere, the papers will predict an immediate victory, and the workers and the soldiers will go back to their jobs. As for Ostnia. . . .

STAHL. You don't understand. You don't want to. You're crazy with conceit! It wasn't just a little local trouble I saw. The officers told me that only Frommer's 18th route army is still completely loyal. I tell you, it means civil war!

VALERIAN. Very well. Suppose it does. Do you seriously think that a rabble of half-baked townees and farm labourers without any officers can stand up against Frommer, who is certainly the best general we've got? I'm afraid they'll be sorry they were ever born. Frommer's not a kind old gentleman, and has rather old-fashioned ideas about the sanctity of private property.

STAHL. It's no use arguing. I know what I saw. They tore the tabs off a colonel and shot him in the stomach before my eyes. It was horrible. This is the end.

VALERIAN. If you think so, then it's no good my talking, is it? I'm sorry that our long partnership should come to such a sudden conclusion.

STAHL. But what are you going to do?

VALERIAN. What should I do? Stay here, of course.

LESSEP. Mr Valerian—What's the use? I beg you to go.

VALERIAN. My dear Lessep, do not alarm yourself. I shall not ask you to stay here with me. Indeed, I order you to accompany Mr Stahl. You would not be the least use to me just now—merely a hindrance. Take him, Stahl, with my warmest recommendation.

178

STAHL. Valerian, this is suicide. Within twenty-four hours there'll be street fighting here. You know as well as I do who they will try to murder first.

VALERIAN. We shall see. If it gets too uncomfortable I suppose I shall have to join Frommer for a while, though I shall dislike that intensely. The man's a bloodthirsty old bore.

LESSEP [*beginning to cry*]. I can't leave you here, Mr Valerian.

VALERIAN. Oh yes, you can. Quite easily. . . . Please spare me these heroics, they do not become you.

STAHL [*looking at his watch*]. Heavens, it's late. We must go at once. If we can't cross the frontier before dawn, we may be fired at. Valerian, for the last time; will you come?

VALERIAN. No.

STAHL. Very well, then. . . . Goodbye.

VALERIAN. Goodbye, my dear Stahl. I shall look forward to your letters about the evils of South America. Please remember me to your wife.

LESSEP [*sobbing*]. Goodbye, Mr Valerian.

VALERIAN. Before we part, Lessep, I've one more job for you. Buy Mr Stahl a new hat.

STAHL [*with a burst of nervous impatience, to* LESSEP]. For God's sake, man, come—if you're coming! Don't waste your pity on him. He's mad!

[*Exit* STAHL *and* LESSEP, *R.*]

VALERIAN. There goes marriage! Poor Stahl! Always the subordinate, staggering under the luggage of a social-climbing wife and a playboy son. . . . He'll dislike South America even more than I should. . . . I wonder if he secretly hopes to be taken back, if things go right, here? If he does, he's mistaken. The family is a charming institution, but one has to pay for it. I don't like deserters.

[*Takes up house-telephone.*]
Hullo. . . . Hullo. . . .

[*Goes to door, L., opens it and calls.*]
Schwarz!

[*No answer. Crosses to door, R., opens it and calls.*]
Schwarz! Frederick! Louis! Kurt!

179

[*No answer. Comes back to centre of stage.*]

Bolted. . . . Well, I can't blame them. . . . Gone to a demonstration, I suppose, to shout stickjaw slogans with the
rest, and listen to their gibbering prophets who promise
the millennium in a week.

[*Goes to window.*]

You poor fish, so cock-a-hoop in your little hour of
comradeship and hope! I'm really sorry for you. You don't
know what you're letting yourselves in for, trying to beat
us on our own ground! You will take to machine-guns
without having enough. You will imagine that, in a
People's Army, it is against your principles to obey orders
—and then wonder why it is that, in spite of your superior
numbers, you are always beaten. You will count on foreign
support, and be disappointed, because the international
working-class does not read your mosquito journals. It
prefers our larger and livelier organs of enlightenment,
which can afford snappier sports news, smarter features,
and bigger photographs of bathing lovelies. We shall
expose your lies and exaggerate your atrocities, and you
will be unable to expose or exaggerate ours. The churches
will be against you. The world of money and political
influence will say of us: 'After all, they are the decent
people, *our* sort. The others are a rabble.' A few of the
better educated may go so far as to exclaim: 'A plague on
both your houses!' Your only open supporters abroad will
be a handful of intellectuals, who, for the last twenty years,
have signed letters of protest against everything from
bi-metallism in Ecuador to the treatment of yaks in
Thibet. . . .

[*As he speaks these last lines, he returns to the desk
and helps himself to a sandwich from a plate which is
lying there. Enter Storm-Trooper* GRIMM, *very quietly,
L.* VALERIAN *turns and starts slightly, on seeing him.*]

VALERIAN. To what do I owe this unexpected pleasure?
GRIMM. I startled you, didn't I?

VALERIAN. Yes, for a moment, I confess you did.

GRIMM. That's what I wanted.

VALERIAN. You came up the back staircase? How did you get in?

GRIMM. The doors are standing open.

VALERIAN. My servants have all run away, it seems.

GRIMM. I knew that. I met one of them in the city.

VALERIAN. So you came to keep me company? Most considerate. . . . You've brought a message, I suppose?

GRIMM. Yes. I've brought a message.

VALERIAN. Excellent. Does the Leader want me to join him?

GRIMM. My message isn't from the Leader. But you may join him. Sooner than you think.

VALERIAN. This all sounds very mysterious. . . . Where is he now? Still in the capital? Or has he gone to Frommer? [GRIMM *does not answer*.] Come, come! We haven't the whole night to waste!

GRIMM. What I have to say to you won't take long.

VALERIAN. So much the better. . . . But first let me offer you one of these excellent sandwiches. . . .

> [*Moves his hand towards the plate*. GRIMM *whips out a pistol and covers him*.]

GRIMM. Keep away from that telephone!

VALERIAN [*after recovering from the shock*]. My dear child, you mustn't wave that thing about! It might go off.

GRIMM. Get back over there. Against the wall.

VALERIAN [*obeying*]. You little fool! It was the Leader who told you to do this, I suppose?

GRIMM. The Leader will never tell me to do anything, again. If you want him, go and look in his study. You'll find him with his face on the table, and twenty bullets in his back, and the blood all over that fine Turkey rug you gave him. . . .

VALERIAN. So? My dear boy, do stop trembling and slobbering at the mouth in that disgusting manner! To tell you the truth, your news doesn't surprise me quite as much as you'd suppose. I always suspected that you and your gang

181

of hooligans would rat, when you thought the time had come. Only, the time *hasn't* come, you see. That's where you show a deplorable lack of political foresight. . . .

GRIMM. I didn't come here to talk about the Leader.

VALERIAN. I can very well imagine why you came here, my murderous little gunman. Having lost one master, you're in search of another. . . . Well, as it happens, I can use you quite conveniently. . . . You have a car with you, I suppose?

GRIMM. What if I have?

VALERIAN. And plenty of petrol? Petrol, in these days, is worth rubies. My chauffeur seems to have disappeared. I want you to drive me to General Frommer's headquarters, at once.

GRIMM. And if I refuse?

VALERIAN. Oh, I hardly expect you to refuse. . . . After your little shooting-party, I've no doubt that you and your colleagues stuffed your pockets with all the bank-notes in the Leader's safe? You're feeling quite rich? Well, let me tell you that, across the frontier, where you will be obliged to travel, very fast and soon, those notes are practically worthless. . . . Now I am prepared to give you ten thousand gold francs. . . .

GRIMM. I don't want your money!

VALERIAN. Fifteen thousand! [GRIMM *is silent.*] Twenty thousand! [GRIMM *is silent.*] Oh, you needn't be suspicious! They're really here, in this room, in a safe behind the panelling. . . . I'm ready to trust you, you see. Aren't you being rather unwise to refuse? Think of the alternative. If Frommer's men catch you—as, without my protection, they probably will—you will be hanged, or possibly burnt alive.

GRIMM. Valerian, the first time we met you thought you recognized me.

VALERIAN. And you assured me that it was impossible.

GRIMM. I was lying.

VALERIAN. So? Your candour does you credit.

GRIMM. Don't you want to know my name.

VALERIAN. Yes. I think you really do owe me an introduction.

GRIMM. It's Grimm.

VALERIAN. Grimm? Grimm? There are so many Grimms in this country. . . . I seem to remember something. . . .

GRIMM. Five years ago, a boy got a job in your office. A week later, some stamps disappeared. He was the latest employee, so they dismissed him, on suspicion. He appealed to you. You said that you could not reverse your head clerk's decision, and that, in any case, guilty or not, an example must be made. . . .

VALERIAN. Ah, I remember now! An unfortunate case. . . . Well, it may please you to know that the head clerk himself was dismissed a few weeks afterwards. He had been cheating us for years.

GRIMM. Yes, I knew that, too.

VALERIAN. I am delighted to be in a position to make you some tardy amends. . . . Shall we say twenty-five thousand?

GRIMM. You said: 'An example must be made.'

VALERIAN. Yes. And I should say the same today.

GRIMM. You haven't changed, Valerian. I'm glad of that. I was afraid. . . .

VALERIAN. Fascinating as these reminiscences are, don't you think we had better be starting? We can continue this discussion much more conveniently in your car.

GRIMM. I took a lot of trouble to get that post in your office. I had to have it. I had to see what you were like—the man who sent my parents to their graves.

VALERIAN. My dear boy, this is sheer persecution mania! You should see a doctor. I assure you that I never set eyes on either of your parents in my life!

GRIMM. No, you never set eyes on them. Probably you never set eyes on any of the people who kept those little shops along Grand Avenue. But your big store undersold them, and ruined them all. My father went bankrupt. He shot himself. My mother died soon after.

VALERIAN. I am truly sorry to hear it.

GRIMM. When I was sacked from your office, without references, I couldn't get a job. One day, I was sitting in the park, your park; I hadn't eaten anything for twenty-four hours. There was a meeting going on; a speaker from the Leader's Party. I listened. A night or two later, I heard the Leader himself. He told us how he would smash the big businesses, the chain-stores, the Valerian Trust. He told us how he would help the small men, people like my father. I believed him. I joined the Party. . . . And then came the National Revolution. We were in power. And it was all lies. The Leader betrayed us. When I realized that, I knew what I had to do. Never mind. That score was settled, at last—tonight. . . .

VALERIAN. Most interesting. . . . And now, may I ask, why do you come here to tell me all this?

GRIMM. I have come to give you a message. A message from my father and mother, and all those others. . . .

VALERIAN. And the message is——?

GRIMM. You must die.

VALERIAN. I must die. . . . How curious. . . .

GRIMM. Say your prayers, Valerian. If you know any.

VALERIAN. How very curious this is! It's quite true. *You* are actually able to kill *me*! And you will! Oh, I don't doubt you're in earnest. I know that pale, hatchet-faced look of yours. . . . When I said that I recognized you, I meant, perhaps, that I recognized that look. I recognized Death. We all know him by sight.

GRIMM. Kneel down, damn you! Pray! Pray for forgiveness! Squeal for your life! Kneel, you swine!

VALERIAN. No, my little man. There you are asking too much. I'm afraid I can't give you the pleasure of humiliating me. It simply isn't in you. Be content with what you have. You can kill the great Valerian. What a treat! Don't tremble so, or you'll miss me altogether and hit that statuette, which would be a real disaster. Come on. Don't be afraid. I am waiting. Shoot.

GRIMM [*panting, near to collapse*]. I—I can't!

VALERIAN. You can't? Ah, now, I'm afraid, you're beginning to bore me. I over-estimated you, you see. I have no interest in weaklings.

184

GRIMM. Get out of my sight, do you hear? Get out!

VALERIAN. Not so fast. You and I have still a good deal to talk about. . . . Put that pistol away and get yourself a drink. You look as if you were going to faint.

GRIMM. Get out, I tell you!

VALERIAN. You think, perhaps, that you might screw up the courage to shoot me in the back? I shall give you no such opportunity. I am quite well aware of the power of the human eye. . . . Now, do pull yourself together. Put it away and let us talk.

[GRIMM *does not move.*]

VALERIAN. Very well. Have it your own way. I can be as patient as you. Probably more so. I think you'll soon get tired of this nonsense. [*A pause.*] Let us pass the time agreeably. Shall I tell you about my crimes? The number of widows I have starved to death? The babies I have trampled under foot? Do I appear to you as a monster with horns? I suppose I do. How strange. . . . Here we are, united, for the moment, by a relationship more intimate than the most passionate embrace, and we see each other as mere caricatures. . . . Are you a human being, too, under your dangerous little reptile skin? No doubt. Have you a sweetheart? I don't think so. In any case, you would soon lose her. Your dreary death-cult is hardly likely to amuse a young lady. . . . Tell me about your mother, though. That's always interesting. I expect you were an only child. Her pet. Born rather late in the marriage. The son who was to achieve wonders. What did she teach you, at nights, beside the cot? What did she whisper?

GRIMM [*screams and shoots*]. Leave my mother alone, you bastard!

[*He fires three more shots into* VALERIAN'S *prostrate body, kicks it savagely, looks wildly round the room, and rushes out, R.*]

CURTAIN

185

(BEFORE THE CURTAIN)

[*The five male members of the chorus represent the typical readers of five English newspapers. They should be dressed according to their shades of political opinion. Thus, the* FIRST READER *has a conservative, highly respectable government paper, the* SECOND *a violently reactionary, more popular paper, with pictures, the* THIRD *a liberal paper, the* FOURTH *a communist paper. The* FIFTH READER, *who is trembling all over, is studying one of those sensational and alarming news-letters which give the 'low-down' on the international situation. Each reader is seated. A spotlight rests on each in turn, as he reads his passage aloud.*]

FOURTH READER. Workers rising everywhere. Fascist Collapse.

SECOND READER. General Frommer confident of victory over Reds.

FIRST READER. Tarnberg believed captured by insurgents. Government forces retire on Konia.

SECOND READER. Red Terror in Tarnberg.

THIRD READER. People's Army successful. White troops in retreat.

FOURTH READER. Workers deal smashing blow to international Fascism. Tarnberg cheers march of heroes.

FIFTH READER. From a source usually reliable, we hear that Markov, the Ostnian General, has secretly left Paris to join Westland's General Frommer as military adviser. Subscribers will recall that Markov has long been a valued friend of Frommer's beautiful blonde wife. As told in number 256 of our bulletin, their friendship had a romantic beginning during the Salzburg festival, two years ago, when the gallant Ostnian rescued Her Ladyship's poodle, Jimmy, from a baroque fountain.

THIRD READER. It is important for us to realize that the People's Army is supported not only by the extreme Left, but by all the Liberal and progressive elements in Westland. If they

186

win, Westland will once more take her place among the Democratic countries.

SECOND READER. Inhuman cruelties by Reds. Bishop boiled alive. British governess' terrible experience.

FOURTH READER. Mass executions in Kresthaufen. Fascist thugs machine-gun women and children.

FIFTH READER. An interesting sidelight on relations between Frommer and the City is thrown from Mayfair. Lady Corker, well-known local right-wing socialite, gave an alfresco supper-party on Thursday last, at which the Westland Ambassador was guest of honour. In the charades which followed, His Excellency and the Chairman of the Anglo-Saurian Oil Co. made a sensation as Darnley and the Queen of Scots.

SECOND READER. Church denounces Communism. World-wide day of prayer ordered for better industrial relations.

THIRD READER. Christianity and Socialism should be allies, says East-End Vicar.

FIRST READER. Tension in Europe increases. Prime Minister to announce British plan for mediation.

SECOND READER. No Bolshevism in Europe, say Anti-Comintern Powers. War material pouring in to Reds from Russia.

FOURTH READER. International Fascism alarmed. Foreign tanks to crush Westland workers.

THIRD READER. Intervention threatened by totalitarian states. League summoned.

FIRST READER. There is an increasing danger of Europe splitting into two irreconcilable camps. To this, the Englishman, with his love of liberty and his distrust of cast-iron ideologies, is tempted to retort, in the words of our national poet: 'A plague on both your houses!'

FIFTH READER. From War Office sources, comes the news that the outbreak of world war cannot possibly be delayed beyond the middle of March. . . . [*Covers his face with his hands.*] Oh dear! Oh dear! Oh dear!

BLACK OUT

ACT III

SCENE III

[*The stage quite bare, with the light-circle, as in the dream-scene in Act II, Scene I. But with this difference: in the extreme corners of the stage, L. and R., are two dimly illuminated beds, containing motionless, unrecognizable figures, over which, in each corner, a doctor and a nurse are bending. These parts are doubled by the actors playing* DR THORVALD *and* HILDA THORVALD, *L.; and* COLONEL HUSSEK *and* MRS VRODNY, *R. There is a screen at the head of each bed.*]

LEFT DOCTOR. Yes, Sister? What is it?

LEFT NURSE. This chest-wound case, Doctor. He's had another haemorrhage.

LEFT DOCTOR. Let me see. . . . Hm. . . . There's nothing I can do, I'm afraid. He's sinking. What's his name?

LEFT NURSE. Eric Thorvald, Doctor.

LEFT DOCTOR. Poor fellow. Knew his father slightly. Clever man. Bit conceited.

RIGHT DOCTOR. What's her name?

RIGHT NURSE. Anna Vrodny. One of our best nurses. Do you think she'll pull through, Doctor?

RIGHT DOCTOR. Not a chance. She won't last the night. Move her out as soon as it's over, Sister. We're terribly short of beds.

[ERIC *and* ANNA, *dressed and made up exactly as in Act II, Scene I, emerge from behind the screens at the heads of their respective beds, and advance into the light-circle. The beds fade into darkness.*]

ERIC. Anna, is that you?

ANNA. Yes, Eric.

ERIC. Come closer. I can't see you clearly.

ANNA. Where are you? Your voice sounds so faint.

ERIC. Standing at the barricade
The swift impartial bullet
Selected and struck.
This is our last meeting.
ANNA. Working in the hospital
Death shuffled round the beds
And brushed me with his sleeve.
I shall not see you again.

[*A distant noise of shots and shouting.*]

ANNA. Will people never stop killing each other?
There is no place in the world
For those who love.
ERIC. Believing it was wrong to kill,
I went to prison, seeing myself
As the sane and innocent student
Aloof among practical and violent madmen,
But I was wrong. We cannot choose our world,
Our time, our class. None are innocent, none.
Causes of violence lie so deep in all our lives
It touches every act.
Certain it is for all we do
We shall pay dearly. Blood
Will mine for vengeance in our children's happiness,
Distort our truth like an arthritis.
Yet we must kill and suffer and know why.
All errors are not equal. The hatred of our enemies
Is the destructive self-love of the dying,
Our hatred is the price of the world's freedom.
This much I learned in prison. This struggle
Was my struggle. Even if I would
I could not stand apart. And after
Sighting my rifle for the necessary wrong,
Afraid of death, I saw you in the world,
The world of faults and suffering and death,
The world where love has its existence in our time,
Its struggle with the world, love's source and object.
ANNA. I saw it too.

189

Working in the wards
Among the material needs of the dying
I found your love
And did not need to call you.

ERIC. We could not meet.

ANNA. They were too strong.
We found our peace
Only in dreams.

ERIC. As irresponsible and generalized phantoms
In us love took another course
Than the personal life.

ANNA. In sorrow and death
We tasted love.

ERIC. But in the lucky guarded future
Others like us shall meet, the frontier gone,
And find the real world happy.

ANNA. The place of love, the good place.
O hold me in your arms.
The darkness closes in.

[*The lights fade slowly. Background of music.*]

ERIC. Now as we come to our end,
As the tiny separate lives
Fall, fall to their graves,
We begin to understand.

ANNA. A moment, and time will forget
Our failure and our name
But not the common thought
That linked us in a dream.

ERIC. Open the closing eyes,
Summon the failing breath,
With our last look we bless
The turning maternal earth.

ANNA. Europe lies in the dark
City and flood and tree;
Thousands have worked and work
To master necessity.

ERIC. To build the city where

190

The will of love is done
And brought to its full flower
The dignity of man.

ANNA. Pardon them their mistakes,
The impatient and wavering will.
They suffer for our sakes,
Honour, honour them all.

BOTH. Dry their imperfect dust,
The wind blows it back and forth.
They die to make man just
And worthy of the earth.

CURTAIN